HOW TO CHOOSE PEACE:
ONE SECOND AT A TIME

HOW TO CHOOSE PEACE:
ONE SECOND AT A TIME

VISHALI SHAHIN, B.S., R.N.

ONE-SECOND PUBLISHING
SEDONA, ARIZONA

HOW TO CHOOSE PEACE:
ONE SECOND AT A TIME

by Vishali Shahin

© 2024 Vishali Shahin
SedonaHealingJourney.com

Published by One-Second Publishing in
affiliation with Fearless Literary Services

ISBN: 979-8-218-45833-1

LIBRARY OF CONGRESS CONTROL NUMBER:
2024915074

COVER DESIGN:
Vishali Shahin & D. Patrick Miller

PRODUCTION & MANAGEMENT
D. Patrick Miller • Fearless Literary
www.fearlessbooks.com/Literary.html

TABLE OF CONTENTS

The Guest House
- RUMI -

This being human is a guest house.
Every morning a new arrival.
A joy, a depression, a meanness,
some momentary awareness comes
as an unexpected visitor.
Welcome and entertain them all!
Even if they're a crowd of sorrows,
who violently sweep your house
empty of its furniture,
still, treat each guest honorably.
He may be clearing you out
for some new delight.
The dark thought, the shame, the malice,
meet them at the door laughing,
and invite them in.
Be grateful for whoever comes,
because each has been sent
as a guide from beyond.

BEGINNING

I COULDN'T MOVE. Nothing was getting me off this couch. Slumped, blank, thought-free, in the nurses' lounge. This was yet another day, one in the many years of overwhelming stress. I wasn't even able to get up to go home.

Hours had passed since my shift had ended. I remained motionless, trapped in a state of numbness. Another nurse entered the lounge, her steps slowing as she registered my vacant stare.

"Are you okay? Are you alright?" she asked with genuine concern. I glanced up at her, the spell finally broken. I gave a feeble "Yes, I'm fine," and realized I had to get out of there. I drove home through the rain, still numb. The only thing I could do was seek refuge in the hot tub of my apartment complex.

Alone, silent, in the rain, balancing an umbrella in the hot tub. Mountains surrounding the apartment were beautiful, as was the sunset. But at that moment, 35 years of unwavering dedication to nursing vanished. I had to leave the profession.

Even though I'd been meditating for several years when I decided to leave nursing, I'd always kept myself too busy and distracted to live by the teachings I was exposed to. I really didn't know what was meant by the 'inner world.'

I'd meditate, expecting some world-shifting revelation. Disappointment invariably followed, as I noticed my mind was busy at worst, or partially quiet at best.

Your mind is the inner world. What you're doing with your mind — what you tell yourself, creates your inner state. We react to whatever the mind has grabbed onto. Whether that's peace or fear, it changes your outer experience of life and contributes to everyone else's experience as a whole.

In this book, you'll learn the workings of the fear-driven ego-mind and its ploys to distract you. Simple processes are included to help you discover how to be your true peaceful self in the midst of the ego's world. Included too are exercises and meditations which make it possible to release, let go and be more free on the inside. These tools can easily be incorporated into your daily life, to catch the ego at its game. Then you can choose peace, over and over again, whenever that peace is threatened by ego-habits.

There are a number of teachings from *A Course in Miracles* (ACIM).* ACIM isn't a religion, rather a self-study course on undoing the ego-mind. The Course shows students how to remove blocks to the awareness of love's presence. On your spiritual path, it's crucial to realize there's another way of seeing and thinking.

In reality there's nothing but love's presence. Yet love, which is our true core, is covered over by the experience of separation. The ego is really nothing more than a belief in separation; we *believe* we have separated from love, or God, when we haven't. Beliefs are powerful!

Undoing of the ego-mind is our spiritual work, revealing the absolute love at our core. However, love's presence is covered up by our insistence that this world, driven by ego beliefs, *is* the real world.

This includes believing we are this physical body, issued at birth, and nothing else. How do you let go of something you believe you are?

Just one second at a time.

* Foundation for Inner Peace, A Course in Miracles: Combined Volume, 3rd edition. (Mill Valley, CA: Foundation for Inner Peace, 2007) ACIM.org

CHAPTER 1

Here You Are Again. Now What?

*Being at ease with not knowing is crucial
for answers to come to you.*
- ECKHART TOLLE -

I WOKE UP enraged. I woke up angry a lot back in my early twenties. Nothing was ever right. I always saw things from a cup half-empty perspective — or more truthfully, my perspective was the glass was bone dry and dusty. I couldn't blame it on my age since I knew a lot of twenty-somethings who were happy and doing great things.

Even though the birds were singing that morning in Syracuse, New York, and the sun was out (a local rarity), I woke up to the familiar feeling of dread. I had recently graduated from Syracuse University School of Nursing. Those years in school kept me too busy to remember how unhappy I was on the inside; now that I worked as a nurse I found fulfillment and connection on the job. But I didn't have it in my personal life. As a matter of fact my motto was "Life sucks and then you die." And I meant it.

This particular morning's rage led quickly to a fight with

my mother. Then my sister Christine showed up and I started fighting with her. I had plans to visit a friend, someone with whom I expected to find some respite from the craziness, but within a few minutes we were fighting too. Overwhelmed with emotion, I yelled at my friend, "I'm fighting with my mother, my sister, and now you! What's wrong with everyone?"

Her reply was simple and direct. "Gee, I wonder what the common denominator is?"

Oh! *I* was the common denominator. That simple statement turned everything around. What was going on *with me*? I was stunned into silence. Until self-awareness dawns on us we all think the world is happening *to* us, leading us to act like victims. Even though each of us is the lead character in our life story, somehow it's all just happening *to* us.

At the time I was in a bad mood about 95% of the time. When the clouds parted I'd feel relief from all the heaviness, but it usually didn't last long — just long enough for me to take a breath. I had no idea I was keeping this darkness intact with my unexamined thoughts and feelings, and my propensity to blame anything that moved.

The idea I had anything to do with how I was feeling got me a bit upset. "NOW what do I do?" There was a glimmer of hope though. My older sister, who had four kids all under 6 years old at this time, told me she chanted 'OM' to her babies to get them to go to sleep. Clearly she was a spiritual person who had answers and would easily be able to answer any of my questions. I visited her on her rural, quiet upstate New York farm. With the peace of nature all around her, I figured she had to be connected to God. I was desperate for answers to relieve my suffering.

One day, we took a walk along the field by her house. Outdoors, I could breathe. Summoning up my courage, I said, "Chris, what are the laws of the universe?" I fully expected an answer which would alleviate my suffering. Instead, my sister stopped dead, stared silently at me for a moment, and then said, "How the hell would I know?" (Not that anyone could answer a question like that.)

Okay then, so much for that; I wasn't going to get answers from her. I was in a panic, realizing there was no one around me who knew the truth. Even my father, an Eastern Orthodox priest, couldn't help me. (In Eastern Catholicism priests are allowed to get married before taking their final vows.) The church was full of dogma, and my dad seemed to know nothing more than the rest of us.

CHAPTER 2

This Is What's Running The Universe?

You have to grow from the inside out. None can teach
you, none can make you spiritual. There is no other
teacher but your own soul.
— SWAMI VIVEKANANDA -

ACH OF US has a story, and we're constantly creating more stories full of drama and suffering. Enmeshed in our own melodramas, it's usually not until we've reached a certain threshold of pain when we think, 'There's gotta be another way.' We're finally ready for change. That one thought opens the door to a higher awareness, and new ways of thinking and being.

However, on our way to our own inner peace, we can get stuck in wanting everybody else to change first. There may not be a recognition the disharmony is coming from our own perception. So we go on to point out every single fault of our parents, spouses, kids, co-workers and on and on. When really they're just reflecting back to us what's inside us.

The reason it's impossible to make someone else change, no matter how many seeds of good intention you try to plant in them, is because they have to reach their own realization, as we have, that they've had enough. It takes a lot to truly want to let go of one's way of thinking. We want others to change so we don't have to do the inner work. Many won't have that recognition in this lifetime. Besides, why do we want other people to stop acting the way they do? It's because *we're* uncomfortable with them. We want them to change so we can be happy. Good luck with that, cuz that ain't gonna happen. Let's just start with being at peace. Start there. Let people do what they do, and we get to change our perception.

Look at the suffering and chaos in the world today — people spewing hatred and fear, masses struggling to barely survive, others fighting back, while a handful of people seem to be the ones controlling events. History recounts war after war, civilizations coming and going, horrific events and genocides. Is this who we are? Really? Thank God the answer to that is "NO."

I was raised to fear a punishing God who'd burn me in hell for not doing what He wanted (perfectly, by the way). *Seriously? This is what's running the Universe?* I've since realized it's the ego's version of God, running the ego's universe of fear, separation and hatred. We think this earth is our true reality... the kind of reality that will make you wake up enraged and terrified on a daily basis.

Many spiritual paths say God created this world; without saying why. That's what I was taught. Years later I found Eastern viewpoints which said God created this world purely to express Itself (God-Self), to know Itself. It never made sense to me: if God was perfect love, how could He be so punitive and hateful, especially to the degree we see on this planet? It seemed sadistic to create a world of hatred in order to know love. The idea of God creating duality seemed antithetical to the essence of God.

We accept this idea without question since we can clearly see the duality of love and hate in this world. We're not really quite sure how we got here, so we just agree. The idea is too huge for the human mind.

The whole God-created-a-fearful-world-thing came crashing down for me (thank God), when I found A Course in Miracles (ACIM or the Course). The Course says there was a tiny tick of time when a thought arose, and instantly vanished, of what it would be like to be separate from God: "Into eternity where all is One, there crept a tiny mad idea at which the son of God remembered not to laugh."[1] That is, we forgot to laugh at the absurdity of the idea of separation. To be separate from our source is actually impossible.

Instead we believed it wholeheartedly and created this world where the ego puts its value system of separation in the place of God. Then the ego acts like it knows what's best for everyone, by the way. The ego values greed, self-defense, and self-serving righteousness. All of which are defenses against recognizing the guilt ego feels for believing it could separate from God. The ego only knows what it wants, and that is to offload the guilt. NOW.

Ego's chief defense is to blame anyone and anything else for every possible problem. Including spouses, children, parents, political figures, and governments. If it moves — blame it. This happens because we feel guilt and shame for separating from God (no, we didn't) and deserve to be punished (no, we don't).

In reality there's only the one mind of God, comprising perfect love, unity, and oneness.

The ego-mind, freaking out over its belief of separation from perfect peace, and its fear of retribution, fragmented into billions of pieces (bodies) to hide from the guilt. But since the guilt was still present, it needed a further plan, and that was to project this guilt onto 'others' by blaming them.

The next logical question could be, "If God is perfect oneness, how could a thought of separation even arise?" The answer from the Course is: "Why would you ask how something seemed to happen a long time ago, when you're still choosing it now?" We're choosing our falsely separated state constantly, second by second.

This world of ego thoughts is not the real world. The real world isn't a place, it's a state of being. Yet it's an elaborate story we find ourselves in. Each time we slip back into believing the ego's unruly voice, fear takes over and we think our connection to God is broken. What we aren't remembering in those moments is that fear is a choice for separation. We never actually left God. But it sure feels like it. So goes the power of belief.

Yet it's actually simple to choose God, if seldom easy. As the Course says, it takes a little willingness. That little willingness can be exercised just one second at a time. It's also what the Course calls the Holy Instant, that moment when you catch yourself in your conditioned mind and choose again.

For decades I really didn't understand what being identified with the ego meant, since I thought all my thoughts were coming from 'me.' How do you dis-identify with something you think IS you? For years I was told that we are too identified with the ego, but no one said how not to be. I felt these thoughts and feelings were me. It wasn't until I read Michael Singer's book, *The*

Untethered Soul, that I discovered how to look at the ego-mind as apart from myself. In the chapter 'The Inner Roommate,' Singer asks if we were to externalize and personify the ego, would we want to hang out with it — someone who only has negative, angry and hateful things to say?

The answer is always a resounding "NO". The ego never has uplifting things to say, so unless you enjoy the angst, why would you hang out with it? Yet we do. We listen to these subconscious patterns that run (ruin) our lives.

For the fun of it, I did imagine putting the ego-mind 'outside' of me and personifying it. I gave it the name Chatty Cathy, (she talks too much). It's a funny thing to do, but it's a metaphor which works. Knowing this ego isn't the real me is helpful in giving me, the decision-maker (that part of the mind that decides where to put my attention), the extra second needed to choose my Higher Self. It's a way to interrupt the ego, breaking its thought-patterns and changing the mind's direction. Very helpful tool when I get too caught up with life's stories.

Many people say the ego-mind does a lot of great things in their lives. This is another trick for us not to look at this thought system closely. All of us vacillate between our ego-mind and our Higher Self. When things work out well in your life, it's because you were with your right-minded thoughts of God.

In Reality There's Only One Mind

In reality there is no separate ego. There's only our bias for drama or our decision for peace. There's only one mind, but what are we doing with it? The Course would say wrong-minded thoughts take us in the direction of the ego-mind, and right-minded thoughts take us to clarity and peace. This isn't about being right or wrong in the punitive sense we grew up with. Not at all. That's going back to the ego's thought system. Rather it's which inner teacher are you letting direct your mind. One could look at it as choosing high-vibration thoughts over lower-vibration thoughts. No matter how you look at it, which inner voice are you listening to? One inner teacher takes us to peace, the other to angst. The choice has always been ours to make. This is the most important tenet of ACIM. Which inner teacher are we listening to?

CHAPTER 3

Tug Of War

Whatever you resist you become. If you resist anger,
you are always angry. If you resist sadness, you are always
sad. If you resist suffering, you are always suffering... We
think that we resist certain states because they are there,
but actually they are there because we resist them.

- ADYASHANTI -

THERE'S A tug of war going on inside us. We want to feel more positive, yet we're dragged back as if by default into negativity. It seems easier to side with just being miserable than happy. After all, there's so much evidence in the world to support sliding into negativity.

How often do we fight with reality? Reality is whatever is happening in the moment, period. Let's say there's a traffic jam. There's nothing you can do, you're stuck. But what do most people do? They scream and yell and even pound the steering wheel. I know this first hand; I used to do that often, and proficiently by the way. That's fighting with reality. In fact, any contrary opinion you have other than what's happening is fighting with reality.

Whether you like it or not, reality is happening.

If you think something should be different from what it is, you aren't accepting what is. You don't have to condone unacceptable situations. Do what you can to rectify or help a situation. If you are in an abusive relationship, you must find the strength to get out of it. Do what you can to uplift yourself. The ego-mind can get you to stay, on the pretense that you have to be better, or even more spiritually accepting of your fate.

For me, a necessary change was leaving the nursing profession after 35 years; it was no longer a fit for me. As a matter of fact the work was so intense and in some ways abusive. I heard myself say out loud, "If this were a relationship I would leave him." I had to accept the necessity of moving on, instead of continuing to fight against that realization by trying to be 'more spiritual,' and make things work. Nursing had been my identity since age twenty, but I finally let go of the inner battle and allowed myself to be more at peace.

Anger about an unhealthy situation isn't going to change it. The energy of anger can even make it worse as the universe responds to our desire to be enraged, or feel victimized, by giving us more anguish. So we fight against *that* realization as well, feeling angry we have anything to do with any of this. The loop of being stuck continues.

In the early 1990's I lived in an ashram in India where we all did seva, or service. My seva was being a nurse in the clinic. We took turns staying overnight in the clinic in case someone got sick at night and needed something.

I was awakened by a woman in her 70's whose Sanskrit name was Shiva Shakti, an interesting identification as it represents both Shiva, the male aspect of God, and Shakti, the female aspect of God.

The name Shakti represents the dynamic forces that move through the universe. She is the creative and sustaining source energy, giving life and action to Shiva. Being the primordial force of the universe, Shiva is powerful and omniscient. One cannot exist without the other. Together they are the very nature of the universe and everything in it.

Shiva Shakti came into the clinic and the doctors on call admitted her for overnight care. Usually I am very loving and empathetic with my patients, but something about this woman rubbed me the wrong way. She insisted things be done her way, and I was trying to be a professional caretaker. We couldn't see eye to eye, and she was annoying the hell out of me. Egos were flaring, to say the least. Eventually I got her settled in for the night, and I went back to my on-call room, from which I could look in on her throughout the night.

As I sat there alone, I contemplated my experience and the resistance to caring for her. I imagined speaking with God, who said: "So Vishali, what are you up to tonight?" and I laughed, replying "Oh nothing Lord, I'm just fighting with Shiva Shakti." As soon as I heard myself, I gasped — I was literally fighting with God. I was fighting with reality, and to make things worse the universe provided a person who had *both* Sanskrit names of God.

Years later, I remember waking up one morning realizing I had another war dream. I much preferred the dreams of flying in space, or being in the presence of a great master. I always woke up from those dreams filled with energy, and gratitude. Why another battle?

At first I lay there disappointed; I wanted to know I was further along on the path than having inner battles. The fact is we never know where we are on the path. You could be one breath away from absolute inner peace, or not. We just don't know.

Many spiritual paths talk about the split mind, and how it's impossible to serve two masters. These two masters are the ego-mind and God-mind. One mind is the quiet, subtle, knowing voice of God or Higher Self. It has no agenda and no need to repeat itself. When we hear this voice, we know it, we feel it, and sometimes we listen. This is our intuition, and it brings happiness to know that we followed this voice because things work out with ease.

Then there are plenty of times we don't follow our quiet voice, instead listening to the inner drama queen, which is loud, boisterous, and repetitive. It's proficient in getting us confused, distracted, and questioning everything. The ego loves suffering, hatred, and division, and it *does* have an agenda, to be the loudest, most confusing voice in your head. Why? To drown out your still, quiet voice. Why would it have such an agenda? It likes chaos.

Remember, the ego-mind split into billions of forms to hide from the retribution it feels must be coming its way for believing it was separate from God. Consumed with guilt for this idea, blame becomes the chief means of alleviating the perceived suffering. It projects its fear and hatred outward: 'It's not me. It's you. You did this.' The ensuing outcome is chaotic, with so much distraction in the 'outside' world, we don't slow down and look within ourselves. If we were to look at this idea of separation, the ego-mind would have nowhere to hide.

If everyone stopped for a second, realizing: Oh, how I'm feeling is about 'me', not about 'them', we'd stop blaming others. If we did that, we'd have peace on this planet in a nano-second.

At some point in time everyone in this dream world will wake up, just not all at once, and not when *we* want them to. Our job is to wake ourselves up with the help of our Higher Self. The ego-mind's not going to give you peace. You've got to leave this thought system and take your peace. When we don't listen to that subtle voice within, it's not a sin, or right or wrong. It's just a matter of how long you want to continue suffering with a head full of the ego's beliefs. Some beliefs can be recognized through introspection and contemplation. Some are subconscious, and we'll look at how to release conscious and subconscious patterns in a later chapter.

In harmony with Eastern philosophies, ACIM tells us: you are at home in God, dreaming of exile but perfectly capable of awakening to reality.[1] So we're dreaming a dream while safely at home with God (or oneness). Whether this world is called an illusion, as ACIM describes it, or Maya as Hinduism and Buddhism call it, it's a dream, not the real world. Unlike the world we seem to be living in, characterized by constant change and suffering, the real world is of God, unchanging and constant in love and unity. We can start to see the real world just by changing our beliefs about the everyday world. As the Course advises, "Seek not to change the world, but choose to change your mind about the world."[2]

Even quantum physics tells us we're living in an illusion. Physicist Niels Bohr summed it up when he observed, "Every-thing we call real is made of things that cannot be regarded as

real." Albert Einstein pointed out that time and space don't
actually exist.

This understanding is so far beyond our daily experience
we can only grasp it on an intellectual level. Then we move on,
continuing to believe we live in time and space. What can we do?
If we grasped the illusion we're steeped in, then we'd have to ask
the question, "Who are we really?"

Ramana Maharishi, a Hindu sage and meditation master,
taught that everyone could increase their faculty of discrimi-
nation so as to discern the real (the eternal infinite spirit) from
the unreal, (the world we seem to inhabit). Asking yourself:
"Who am I?", is a step away from the ego-mind. It can give you a
second-by-second contemplation that will lead to a release into
God. But you have to step away from the ego merely to ask the
question. The problem is the storyline of the ego driven world
seems so convincingly real.

There's a wonderful story to illustrate the idea of Maya, or
illusion. Lord Shiva and Lord Narayana were taking a walk, and
Lord Shiva got thirsty. He sent Narayana to the well to get him
some water. Happy to serve, Narayana walked toward the well.
While he was there he met a beautiful woman, and they started
to chat.

He fell madly in love with her and decided to marry her. He
asked her father's blessings and the wedding was held. Over the
years they had three children and lived a very happy life. One
year a serious monsoon hit, and the rains wouldn't stop, flood-
ing the town. Narayana's home was destroyed and he found
himself in a raging river with his family. He and his wife were
hanging onto each other and their children. One of the children

was swept away. Distraught, Naryana held tighter to the rest of his family.

Yet, one by one the raging waters swept each child away. His wife was inconsolable, so she let go into the water after her children. Alone now, Narayana began praying in anguish: "Lord look at what's happened here! Where are you? Help me and my family!" Then Narayana heard a voice calling to him. "Narayana! Narayana! Where's my water?"

God is never not here, but always present in our hearts and in our minds. Yet the illusory world can easily sweep away our awareness. We have to choose to remember God, even if it's just for a second. Separation from God never occurred, we are just dreaming it did.

Every single person on this dream planet has the distant memory of being their true Self in God — even those people you find horrible. Sharing our dream of separation, they too are safely at home with God. We are all on our way to remembering home, getting there in our own time.

I was once in a chapel in Sedona filled with visitors from around the world. Outside, the chapel was very busy and people were yakking, taking pictures, and being touristy. Inside the fully occupied chapel, everyone was silent; peace filled the room. As I watched it struck me that everyone, despite my opinions, remembers who they really are. Everyone was connected from their heart to the energy of God. How much we stay in remembrance is up to us.

When we aren't in remembrance, it's because of our identification with the ego-mind. We literally think this voice is us. We say things like "I am angry, I am sad, I am jealous," etc. But who is speaking? If you ask yourself this question, it gives you a pause during which you can choose again. The ego-mind has to be witnessed to be released. Asking yourself, "Who's speaking?" gives you a second to step out of the ego-mind. Once you're out, you're out. Now extend those seconds for as long as you'd like, or can. But you can't let go of something you don't know is there. The ego provides a constant stream of noise loud enough to keep us unaware we have the option of peace. That's why I like the metaphor of placing the ego (Chatty Cathy) next to me. It's an idea which gives me a second to stop and choose again.

The Course asserts, "Ideas leave not their source." The source of all thoughts is either the right-mind or the wrong-mind. Which mind you choose to think with will create the content of that mind's thought system. We think life is happening to us, when in reality it is happening from within us. Where are you putting your attention?

Let's say you wake up one morning and immediately stub your toe, which hurts like hell. You scream and cry and jump around. You're now in a bad mood, crabbing the whole way into the kitchen to make your coffee. You're walking back to your room and spill the coffee, giving you more reason to be miserable. On your way to the car you trip down the stairs and this really upsets you. Once you get to work you're in a bad mood for the office meeting, anxious to get through it. You get down on yourself, thinking you could've done better. Then you go home worried you're going to get fired.

Or: You wake up one morning and immediately stub your toe and it hurts like hell. You scream and cry and jump around. Once the pain subsides you're giggling at yourself for waking up with such a jolt. You let it go and make your coffee without incident, get down the stairs easily, and you give the best presentation of your career at the meeting. The day's going to happen anyway — which inner teacher are you listening to?

Have you ever created an entire hostile story in your head about someone, based on little to no evidence? It's usually self-righteous, melodramatic, flavored with anger, jealousy or fear. Then you find out the truth and the whole fabricated story dissolves, leaving you embarrassed — especially if you've gossiped about it. People spend their whole lives believing made-up stories and stay in their anger for decades. They often die with their resentments intact.

Have you noticed you have the same repetitive thoughts over and over in a day? These recurring thoughts persist for years, creating what we don't want in our experience so that we can blame others for it. According to the Course, "You are much too tolerant of mind wandering, and are passively condoning your mind's mis-creations."[3] We're way too tolerant of the thoughts which arise to distress us. We believe them without even considering what's being said.

The popular New Age teaching is to change your thinking to create the life you want. There's nothing wrong with keeping your thoughts on what you prefer in life. Keeping a more positive outlook will lead you in a more positive and joyful direction. Yet we've all had the experience of wanting something that never manifested. How many people have used the Law of Attraction to become a millionaire? How many people are still not millionaires? What we really do is either think with fear, which creates more fear, or, choose peace, no matter what's happening in our lives. Even if we're choosing peace just one second at a time.

The real challenge is choosing peace whether we get what we *think* we want or not. It's when we're attached and/or disappointed with how things are now, that we suffer. Miscreative thoughts are part of the wrong-minded thought system which feels guilty because of the false belief it separated from God. That's where the idea of a vengeful God comes from, along with the fear He will punish us for leaving. In fact we create our own retribution with various forms of self-punishment, staying unhappy in our stories.

To keep ourselves interested in staying with the wrong mind we also create just enough happiness to engender hope for a better life (but only if we try harder). It's this striving that keeps us involved with our separated delusion. That's the carrot on the stick: "Gosh, life's hard, but it's got to get better. I just need to leave this relationship/ job/place and find a new situation." The problem is that if we haven't let go of identifying with our subconscious thoughts, we'll go on to the next set of circumstances haunted by the same old problems.

There is no retribution in God. Retribution comes from the ego-mind. God is pure love and unity. It's up to us to let go and see everything from a higher perspective. This means whenever you're around anyone, or when you see the news, remember, they're also caught in the belief in separation. They're unaware of their true nature, which is peace. God's always with us, but we have to choose to remember. Being human, we'll often forget — which makes every second of remembering important. All those seconds add up.

We tend to fight with reality more than we care to admit.

Think about what you want to be different in your life. It may be people you react to negatively, or situations you can't stand.

List exactly what you want to be different in your life. There's nothing wrong with making a list. It's all in your head anyway.

_____

_____

_____

Here's your choice: You can spend another 20 years yearning after everything you wrote down, believing it's _required_ for your happiness, or you can look beyond the ego's story and see it from a higher perspective.

ACIM states, "Love holds no grievances."[4] But the ego has plenty of grievances. The goal is not to get rid of them, but look at them and notice who's looking with you. You can choose differently by looking at them _with_ God (the right-mind). There's a cost to holding grievances; "My grievances hide the light of the world in me."[5]

What the Course calls the "holy instant" happens when we shift our attention away from our grievances and onto God. That alone _is_ a miracle. Considering our attachments to certain ideas and beliefs, it absolutely is a miracle to shift our attention away from needing to feel right all the time.

**The real world is the world of peace.
We hide the truth from ourselves by wanting
what the ego wants for us.**

The ego-mind has us convinced that a miracle has to be a huge event in our lives, like a spontaneous healing, winning the lottery, or narrowly escaping misfortune. We may also think it would be miraculous to have all our desires fulfilled exactly as the ego wants. The real miracle is just leaving the ego-mind behind, even for a second.

Look at your list of disappointments or triggers.

How do you feel about them? Frustrated, angry, fearful?

Make another list of your feelings about not having your life be exactly as you'd like.

_____

_____

_____

Sit with these feelings. I know it's not easy. You've heard this before — take a breath and ask: "Who believes this? Who am I really?" Is everything you're listening to really true? Who's speaking? Ego or God?

Is God really saying, "Yup, you screwed up, no wonder you're feeling miserable. You better fix this mess if you want to be enlightened." As funny as that sounds, we can think like that.

As you feel the feelings, you may say a little prayer: "God, please look at these feelings and beliefs with me. I let go of all that I'm buying into." Then stay in the presence of your Higher Self and let the feelings dissolve. If the feelings come up again, take a second to come back to God for another look at them.

Keep choosing a different perspective one second at a time. Again, our spiritual work is the undoing of the ego-mind. This is what I call the One-Second Cure: being easy on yourself and choosing Higher Self, one second at a time. No one lets go of the wrong mind all at once. The ego-mind will try to convince you you've failed just because you haven't let go... *yet.*

A guest on one of my tours was relieved hearing about the One-Second Cure. She told me for the last few weeks she'd held an intention to be kind to a woman at work she couldn't stand. Every day she'd come home from work feeling as if she'd failed, because she still couldn't stand her. Then she figured it out, and very excited she said: "I haven't failed! I just have more seconds to go!"

CHAPTER 4

Hey, Moses Got A Burning Bush —
What About Me?

At any moment, you have a choice, that
either leads you closer to your spirit
or further away from it.
- THICH NHAT HANH -

WANDERING through a bookstore, I stumbled across a book, *The Disappearance of the Universe*. Interesting title. I skimmed a few pages, before putting it back, thinking, I don't need this, I've got a Guru.

A week later, I received an unexpected package from my sister. Yes... the very same sister I asked about the laws of the universe. She sent me *The Disappearance of the Universe*, a book which ultimately answered all my questions. So she *did* finally answer my question, about three decades later! Better late than never. This book led me to ACIM, which I've been studying since 2006.

The undoing of the ego's thought system is required to reveal our true nature. This thought system tells us we're separate from each other, but we're seldom conscious of those thoughts. It's our subconscious patterns which keep us identified with the ego-mind.

Ultimately you've got to become your own teacher, which means doing your own inner work. I used to think going inside only required sitting still for meditation. That may well be part of a practice, but going inside means noticing what beliefs you're allowing to run your life — and then questioning whether those thoughts and beliefs are true.

Do we even know where our thoughts come from? We open our mouths and sounds come out. Who's speaking? If you had to plan your sentences before speaking it would take all day to get a thought out. Thoughts arrive on their own, then the ego-mind claims ownership of them. We have so many thoughts that automatically happen. It's like a 24/7 radio station that switches channels every few seconds. We think this is normal. Well, it is normal from the ego-mind's point of view, until awareness awakens, and we can choose otherwise.

Ego thoughts are designed to keep us stuck in the belief of separation. These include thoughts of judgment, blame, guilt, and fear. These are just a few choices from the ego's play list it uses to keep you believing you're a person with all these problems that are needing to be fixed. The ego-mind wants us to believe not only are we a separate person, but there's something really wrong with us which needs fixing. This keeps us really busy in our lives, trying to become a better person, but never quite good enough.

That's what the ego-mind does, it creates an atmosphere in which we can't recognize the obvious connection we have to God. It convinces us a genuine spiritual experience of divine connection has to be grandiose, otherwise it's nothing.

It can't just be love or peace. That's too simple, because to the ego, love is always dangerous — it contradicts everything whirling around the ego-mind. It knows zero about love, so it distracts us from any relationship we do have with love. Look at the relationships we typically have; it takes a strong commitment to keep them intact. Look at where the conditioned mind comes in and creates drama and separation, leading to resentments and frequently divorce. How many relationships will be better when we catch the ego doing what it does best — it attacks. The ego is 'fight energy.'

When I first went to the ashram, all the displays of love seemed corny. People were sharing heartfelt stories of transformation and devotion. I rolled my eyes at these stories. I felt I was too cool for love. My heart was closed down, I couldn't even recognize love right in front of me. Until we remove the blocks to love's presence, we're stuck with such an egocentric interpretation.

In the Bible there's the story of Moses and the burning bush. As Moses was leading his people out of Egypt, he saw in the desert a burning bush. It caught his attention because the flames weren't destroying the bush. He got closer to the bush and suddenly a booming voice started giving him instruction for the next leg of his journey. God also assured Moses He is always with him. Moses couldn't deny this was an extraordinary spiritual experience. God himself was speaking directly to him. Some spiritual experiences can be this obvious, but most aren't. God's voice can also be very quiet, and subtle.

We expect our spiritual experiences to be as extraordinary as a burning bush, otherwise we negate the obvious. We are so identified with the ego-mind, we don't recognize we're never separate from God. We tend to take for granted the sight of a beautiful flower, or a moment of quiet. That's because the ego-mind knows nothing of beauty or quiet.

During ashram programs there was an emphasis on sharing meditation experiences which I dreaded. This particular path was a path of kundalini awakening. In Eastern spiritual teachings, kundalini is known as the principle within each of us that compels us to evolve and grow spiritually. It can often be a subtle experience which changes your life's direction for the better. It can also be profound as it moves through the body's energy centers, giving some people very dramatic spiritual experiences.

Many people in the ashram had wild, incredible experiences they couldn't wait to share. Since the ego-mind loves to compare, I would lust over everyone's experiences of flying around the universe with God, feeling ecstatic. These people reported visiting other universes, being blown out of their bodies and becoming one with God. It wasn't as if I'd never had significant experiences; they just weren't as dramatic as my ego-mind wanted. From the ego's point of view, the more wild the meditation experience the better. Though these people's experiences were true spiritual experiences, comparison is another trick of the ego to keep us from realizing what's happening *for us*. But the ego loves to compare and keep us imprisoned in a thought system driven by a sense of lack.

Which is exactly what happened to me. During one meditation intensive I fell into a place within me that was "the peace which passeth all understanding" — a peace which was alive and palpable, not of this world. I was surrounded by a thick atmosphere of stillness and a sense of profound protection. There was an absolute certainty God's presence was always with me. It was more real than what I considered reality. I remember thinking, where am I? I felt as though I were in a different place, yet it was within me.

At the end of the program people shared about their cosmic experiences of oneness, and intense experiences of bliss. Instantly my ego-mind started comparing those experiences with mine. It wanted something bigger and better. Within seconds I forgot my revelatory peaceful experience. I never sat down and contemplated what that experience really meant. I allowed the ego to discount it. I wanted a burning bush, something obvious like Moses got. It's important to take the time to honor and contemplate your experiences, even if they seem subtle. Nothing else matters.

Several years after that, I was still putting importance on these kinds of experiences. I decided to take a class to become more psychic, thinking I needed to be more sensitive and open. I arrived a minute late for the class and sat down in the front row. I was impressed with the woman giving the talk and I made an appointment to have a reading from her. When I arrived for my reading she asked me, "What were you doing in my class, why were you there?" All I could say was: "Excuse me?" She went on to say, "When you walked in and sat down you totally unnerved me. You know this stuff, you could teach this stuff!" My only thought was: *Not in this lifetime, lady.*

We all have experiences in other lifetimes we don't need to repeat. She picked up on the idea that I already knew this. Being psychic doesn't equate to being spiritual. A lot of psychic people can do nefarious things with this skill. But if you're psychic *and* spiritual you can use this in service of God.

From the moment I met the Guru there was a deep sense of knowing. For some people this knowing is our experience of remembering the truth. The psychic experiences from other lives didn't have to be expressed again in this lifetime. Everyone will have all kinds of experiences in our numerous lives. None is better than the other, it's all leading us to awakening. But the ego knows when we're closing in on the truth and will use anything to distract us. Comparison is a big one it uses.

Another time at the ashram in India, I had the job of going onto the mobile medical clinic that went to the villages around the ashram, tending to villagers. Many of the western nurses and doctors had this opportunity for doing their service. It was an amazing experience. I loved being around people, and I loved to serve in this way. Meeting the villagers was very different from people of our Western society. They were people who owned almost nothing, most didn't even have shoes. Throughout my time working in the mobile clinic, I felt a profound sense of purpose in providing for them. I felt compassion and love, and a connection to these people as fellow humans, albeit with a very different life than mine.

These villagers had no money to go to hospitals or clinics in their area. In many parts of rural India there were no clinics anywhere. They would walk, some of them for days, from surrounding villages to get treatment for their babies.

One of the ashram staff members was told to come and ask people about their experience of their job (seva/service). She sat with me and asked me about my clinic experience. My mind went immediately to transcendent experiences; I was sure that anything I could possibly tell her about my service was surely too mundane. When she pushed me to share my experiences in the clinic, I had nothing to tell her. My ego-mind made me miss the obvious: that I felt love and connection with the villagers I'd served, which is a spiritual experience. It was a deep, heartfelt experience of love and respect.

Not long after, I remember listening to a friend tell me of his two-week experience of living in oneness. Everyone he'd met was one energy, with no separation from himself; everyone was God. He was blissed out for those two weeks. Then he started talking about what an idiot his neighbor was, and how he couldn't stand him. I asked him respectfully how it was possible to live in a state of oneness for so long and not view his neighbor with more compassion or love. His answer: "Well, I'm not in that state now, am I?"

The world's designed by the ego to keep us intrigued and involved with it. It seems all too normal to slip back into the ego-mind thought system. We'll vacillate between our Higher Self and ego-mind, that's part of the process. We don't have to stay with the ego-mind as long as we used to. We have the power of choice, and we can choose just one second at a time.

ACIM states, "Be vigilant only for God and His Kingdom." [1] Just keep your eye on God. Experiences, whether spiritual or mundane, come and go. But extraordinary experiences are not required for awakening or enlightenment. If you have dramatic or revelatory experiences, contemplate them and be grateful for them, they can help keep our attention on what's really important — just remember if something comes and goes, it's not the real world. What's required for awakening is the undoing of the ego thought system.

Adyashanti, a spiritual teacher, has talked about how we get distracted by spiritual experiences and end up chasing them, instead of undoing the ego-mind. This helped me considerably, as I realized I was chasing experiences instead of keeping my attention on what I really wanted: to know my true nature.

I used to complain that all I got in meditation was a quiet mind. It took me a decade to understand how ludicrous that sounded. "Everyone else got to fly around the universe while all I got was a quiet mind." Sounds like a great logo for a tee-shirt for spiritual vacationers.

I had a guest from New York on one of my tours in Sedona. She was in her seventies. She pointed at me and exclaimed, "I want *you* to give *me* a oneness experience of God!" (Yeah, well I want that too.) I said a silent prayer, something like: 'You brought her here, you better come up with something I can say.' I heard myself ask her: "What are you like in New York?" She said she was closed off, didn't speak with people, and that she was demanding and impatient.

So I asked her: "What are you like in Sedona?" She completely melted and put her hands over her heart. "Oh, in Sedona, everyone is so welcoming and kind. I've had so many meaningful conversations, this place is amazing." I pointed out to her that she was actually *having* a "oneness" experience, regardless of what else she was looking for from me. She was connected to her heart in Sedona. She was looking for the dramatic, while she was missing the obvious. She could take this connection to people back with her to New York.

We've all heard the story of the seeker who goes to the master and demands spiritual knowledge. The master pours the aspirant a cup of tea but doesn't stop pouring, and the cup overflows. The aspirant yells, "Hey you're spilling the tea!" The master replies, "You've come to me with your cup already full, so any knowledge I give you would be wasted. Come back when you've let go of some of your ideas and concepts. Then I can teach you."

The ego-mind has us miss the obvious, so we won't connect with the quiet and stillness within, which is God. It diverts our attention as long as we *allow* it. You have spiritual experiences throughout the day you may take for granted. It's right in front of you.

Foundational Exercise:

Let's do an exercise which is the foundation for your inner work. Sit quietly for a moment, take a deep breath. Exhale and relax. Take a few deep breaths, then gently close your eyes. Now bring up a scene from your life in your mind's eye, something that puts you in a state of peace or awe. It could be watching a sunset or the ocean, or another favorite view in nature.

Describe your scene: Using adjectives like *beautiful, powerful, peaceful,* let the words come flowing out onto the page. Take another deep breath as you continue to connect with your scene.

Write these adjectives down:

_____

_____

_____

What did you describe? You described *yourself*. You described who you really are. This exercise is a reflection of your right-mind. These words are symbols of the real world. The exercise evoked within you what's already there.

This exercise reveals our experiences aren't derived from anything 'outside' us, but from our perceptions. A waterfall, for instance, isn't literally beautiful itself; it's our experience of the waterfall which feels beautiful to us. That is, when something is beautiful to you, your description will actually reveal your inner nature. You extend that perception outward into the world. Any uplifting or expansive thoughts comes from our God-mind, or right-mind.

Another way to say it is, we *are* our Higher Self. When you're connecting to anything in an uplifting manner, you are naturally in your right-mind. When you're feeling bad, you've come back into the conditioned mind. In our moment-to-moment experience, we can begin to see how often we are aligned with the right-mind or wrong-mind.

We have access to all kinds of uplifting experiences all the time, but the ego-mind jumps in and convinces us nothing amazing happens very often. It tells us to wait for the next amazing experience to happen. All the while ensuring that it doesn't happen by tuning us out from what's extraordinary or significant in our everyday life.

So we sit around longing for the next amazing experience to happen. The fact is we have access to God all the time. We just have to choose it.

Caring about someone is a spiritual experience. Being kind is a spiritual experience. Smiling and connecting to your Uber driver is a spiritual experience. Seeing the divine in each other is a spiritual experience. Catching yourself being judgmental can be a spiritual experience, as long as you don't judge yourself for being judgmental. Just observe with God.

Choosing to choose your right-mind over your ego-mind, just one second at a time, is definitely a spiritual practice. It's not like negative thoughts won't show up, because they will. It's what you do with them next which counts. How identified are you with these thoughts? Do you feel these thoughts are who you are? Do you believe them, or is it energy passing through that you've labeled and put in your story?

You can also do this exercise with a memory that gave you a high state of being, like the birth of a child or falling in love. Or getting the promotion you wanted. There was most likely a sense of fulfillment and gratitude. Take away the memory and stay with the feeling state. Again, this feeling state, is who you really are. It's coming *from* you, not *to* you. This is something we have access to all the time. It's always present, it's never not there.

We don't own our Higher Self like we own the ego-mind. If I were to ask you what it's like to be angry, frustrated or worried, you could tell me. You're familiar with how those emotions feel in your body. You own it by saying: "I am angry, I am frustrated, I am worried." But if I ask you what it's like to be magnificent, you'll probably say, "Oh I'm not magnificent." The ego-mind quickly jumps in and denies your higher experience so you don't own it. It lets you talk *about* God, but you don't own it. It keeps you away from the very thing you *are*. That's what it does in all areas of our lives, all day long. The ego-mind jumps in and claims our lives.

When we watch a sunset we often experience a state of awe and reverence. As soon as the sun sets, we're usually off and running to the next distraction. We miss the deeper connection, the whole point of the sunset. And if we do stay quiet after the sun sets for a bit we don't usually connect the moment of reflection to our true Self. We may appreciate the fact that we felt peaceful while watching the sun set. But feelings come and go; the connection you experience is always there. The next time you're in a state of reverence while looking at a sunset, remember you're experiencing *yourself*, not the sunset. Take a second to breathe that in and acknowledge it as your true Self.

When you stop identifying with the ego, (ego exits stage left), you can answer the question, what it's like to be magnificent from Higher Self perception. You'd share what it's like to be magnificent, with humility, since arrogance left the room. You'd be standing in the power of your own magnificence. And own it with dignity.

We tend to bypass spiritual connections available to us throughout the day because we're waiting for something grand. Become familiar with that which is subtle.

**We spend our lives chasing experiences
that always change, but our Higher Self is
constant and steady; it never changes.**

Practice:

Any time you see a beautiful flower, remember someone may be behind you rolling their eyes because they hate that flower. So it's not the flower you're appreciating. Whenever you feel reverence, that reverence *is* you. When you see beauty, you *are* that beauty. Take a second to recognize that, and breathe in the experience of beauty. These are really your right-minded thoughts you are owning as your true nature. Just for a few seconds, *be* that beauty. No one even has to know you're doing it.

You can't let go of wrong-minded thinking from the ego's point of view. Albert Einstein said: "We can't solve our problems with the same level of thinking that created them." To let go of ego thinking, you have to get bigger than the ego. That would be Higher Self/God.

This connection to your Higher Self is the foundation of your life. We start here when we choose the One-Second Cure. Step into whatever your connection is with Higher Self/God, and remember to choose even if it's just for a second.

You can't let go of the ego from the ego's point of view. It won't let go. Keep stepping into your God realization, even for a second, and peace is right there.

Meditation: Owning Your True Self

Take one of the adjectives you listed above.

Recognize you've described a reflection of your true self.

Let this realization flood your entire being.

Breathe in, as if you could breathe up to the top of your head, hold your breath for a second, then exhale.

Relax all the way down into your feet. The energy of your experience is filtering down through every cell. This is you.

If other thoughts come while you're doing this, gently let them go and come back to your breath. Let everything else go. Be in this experience.

Take notice of how it feels to breathe higher experiences into your heart, multiplying this feeling with several in-breaths.

Sit as long as you'd like in quiet, being who you are.

The obvious truth is all around us;
it's just a matter of
remembering to stop, and connect.
Just one second at a time.

CHAPTER 5

Super Hero Action Figure

If you think you're enlightened,
go spend a week with your family.

- RAM DASS -

THE COURSE identifies the body as the "hero" of our dream. While we're self-identifying as a body, anything and everything can be seen as dangerous and harmful. You feel good when the body feels good; you feel upset or miserable when the body doesn't feel well. Almost everything we do serves the maintenance and well-being of the body, and we really do have to take care of it.

It's possible to take care of the body without identifying yourself with it. Do all the things you'd do to stay healthy. A lot can happen to the body. However, as long as you identify with it, you won't know what it means to be invulnerable. True invulnerability means identifying with your 'right-mind,' which leads you to peace.

When we first believed we were separate from God, the ego-mind immediately felt guilty, believing it did something horrible and deserved punishment. The world created by the ego is chaotic and terrifying because it symbolizes what the separation would be like, *if* it were true.

Chapter 13 of the Course says: "The world you see is the delusional system of those made mad by guilt. Look carefully at this world, and you will realize that this is so. For the world is the symbol of punishment, and all the laws that govern it are the laws of death......They appear to lose what they love, perhaps the most insane belief of all. And their bodies wither and gasp and are laid in the ground, and are no more. Not one of them but has thought that God is cruel. If this were the real world, God *would* be cruel." [1]

Sounds intense. But thank God, God isn't cruel. However, the ego is determined to create not only a punitive God but also the idea of us being vulnerable and regularly in danger. One method is using 'attack thoughts', which are any thought that disturbs your inner peace. Lesson 26 in the Course states: "My attack thoughts are attacking my invulnerability." [2] If you feel you need to either attack or defend, you're feeling vulnerable, but that's only when you're identified with the ego-mind. Any judgment you have, is an attack thought because it means you aren't accepting who you *really* are.

When do you judge? Judgment's almost automatic, almost all the time. Say you see a 60-year-old woman with fuchsia spiked hair, strolling down the produce aisle and your immediate reaction is "She's gotta be kidding, she looks ridiculous."

Now when I'm in the produce aisle, I can't help seeing that 60-year-old woman with fuchsia hair, but there's no commentary about her anymore.

A quick process for this would be to realize the thought about the woman is really something about you, that you're projecting onto someone else. Welcome that thought. Look at her again in your mind's eye. This time see her as another aspect of Spirit. Look without judging. When we're triggered by others, it's really because we're upset with ourselves for not being at peace. They too are waking up. We're all on our own timeline. Since it's about our projection, we can utilize whatever comes up to release and return home to the real world.

The more I judge others, the more I'm making the ego's world real. Since the ego-mind wants to offload guilt as quickly as possible, what we're actually projecting outward is coming from our identification and perception from that thought system. Anything you feel about someone else is really about your view in relation to the ego-mind. (It's not about them, and it's not about who you really are.)

When you catch yourself being hard on others, or yourself, stop. Notice you're identifying with being the ego-mind. It's the energy of judgment you're still identified with. 'You' aren't judgmental. It's not wrong for judgment to be there, it's being aware of the ego-mind *trying* to keep you stuck. That's why I like the idea of externalizing the ego — Chatty Cathy. It gives me a second more often, to catch what it's saying more frequently.

Catching 'her' gives me the second I need to disidentify with it. I'm saying catch it more often, more frequently, not saying every time, done perfectly. Bring more awareness one second at a time.

To see everything from "above the battleground," the Course would say, is really being the observer of what's happening. We make everything real when we identify as a body. The body must be protected if 'I' (the body) am threatened in any way. But when we look at it as the observer, we can be above the battleground with a peaceful perspective. There's no need to be defensive in the observer perspective.

People are either expressing love or calling out for love. When we look at life from above the battleground, we can express love by not judging. When we do find ourselves trapped in our ego-mind, then in that moment we too are calling for love. The love we're calling for is our remembrance of God. The good news? When we notice this, shift to the One-Second Cure.

We've traditionally wanted God to come and fix things in our lives. We've made prayers of supplication asking for this dream to be better for us. There's nothing wrong with wanting your life to be a certain way. But we can get stuck into thinking we're not spiritually advanced enough if things don't go our way. It can be a trap thinking we're not connected to God if we don't get what we want. Somehow we have to try harder in order to get things right (from the ego's point of view). See how that can keep us stuck?

Instead of wanting God to fix the problems in the world, (which so far hasn't happened), ask to see things the way Higher Self does. Clear your mind of the ego's perspective so you can see the world from peace. Ask Higher Self to look at the fear, anxiety, judgment, wrong-thinking of any kind with you. It's a second-by-second surrender to seeing things differently.

I had a dream one night. I was looking at a picture hanging on a wall. All the people in the frame were moving, just like pictures in a Harry Potter movie. There were rows of prisoners sitting on benches. Weaving in and out between the inmates was Ramana Maharishi, the Indian sage mentioned earlier. The prisoners' faces looked relaxed, peaceful, as they listened to Ramana. Abruptly, each row of inmates got up and walked back into the prison.

I was staring at the now-empty picture frame when an unknown man appeared from behind me and asked, "So what do you think of the picture?" Tears started to come as I said how sad I was that the inmates were returning to prison. The man emphatically said, "You're too much in the story!" Then I woke up.

In the dream I was judging what I saw, making it real. I didn't think of how fortunate those prisoners were to be with Ramana. Instead I was sad they were in prison. Who was in prison, the prisoners, or me? The prisoners were relaxed and at peace as they were with God himself in the form of Ramana. I was the one in the prison of my own mind.

Too often, we're wedded to the ego-mind's way of looking at things. It's always making sure we buy into the stories we see in front of us, even in night dreams.

The dream reminded me of a time when I had a great connection with a wonderful man. It didn't last, and I was very saddened by it, grieving the loss. Several weeks after this breakup, I bumped into an old friend. (Really, the universe sent him to shake me up.) I poured out my break-up woes, expecting sympathy. Instead, he quietly said, "Wow, Vishali — you jumped right back into Maya" [the illusory world].

My friend was right; hearing his words enabled me to jump out of the illusion. Now, it's not as if I didn't still feel the grief from losing such a fun relationship – but I could finally see that the grief wasn't about that particular man, it was just the energy of grief.

So when my friend pointed out I'd dived back into the illusion, I could see the grief separate from the story. No matter what difficult emotion comes up, the core of it really is our belief in separation. We use the same story in different variations to keep ourselves in Maya. Whatever comes up is something that's blocking love's presence, and thus something to acknowledge and let go of.

I realized I'd wanted that relationship, in that moment more than I wanted to wake up, more than I wanted God. That's how we stay stuck. The ego-mind makes the story seem so real we can't help but stay there, spinning our wheels. For me when the energy of grief resurfaced, I was able to look at the grief with God, *without* the story. In actuality, I was grieving my belief in separation from God. I realized if I were already one with God, I wouldn't be suffering. Even if I just had my attention on God it would be enough. It's not about perfection.

It's perfectly normal to love another person madly and to have a relationship. Remember, just like the exercise in Chapter 4, they've evoked the love in *you* that's already present. However, in the midst of that, it's crucial we keep our eye on the ball of seeing everything here as a tool for awakening. That's the foundation of what the Course calls a "holy relationship" — a relationship in which you're inspired by the mutual decision to focus on letting go of grievances you think are coming from your partner, and grow into love and peace together. This is a conscious and personally responsible relationship of love. Entering into a relationship like this comes from mutual right-minded thinking.

Of course stuff will come up. What bothers you is just not about them.

We tend to get caught in gratifying the ego, but the ego is *never* satisfied; it's an endless black hole. The right-minded approach is to use challenging emotions and circumstances as vehicles for introspection, letting go, and spiritual growth. Love is what you've got, when you're not buying into the ego's stories.

Have you noticed the ego loves to come in and attack your peace even when you're sitting around doing nothing? It's like there's a superhero action figure insisting on your attention at all times. That's another ruse by the ego to keep you in the story by being your personal hero. How often have I had daydreams where I saved the day? Somehow I subdued the rifle-toting bad guy twice my size, and miraculously brought him down. Or I successfully intervened, using only my love and light in a hostage situation. C'mon, really? I'm 5'3", 120 lbs, and I bolt out of the house when a wolf spider is on the wall. (They're really huge!)

It's laughable, but it's thoughts like these running in the subconscious which convince us we're vulnerable and need constant defending. It's what keeps us dreaming a dream of separation: I'm the good guy and I conquered the bad guy.

The best melodrama is when you have a complete conversation in your head with someone who's bothering you, and you go back and forth with what you'd say, then what they'd say. You make all your angry points no one could refute. And bingo, you win! You never do have that conversation, but it kept you engaged, and not in peace.

If you don't think you do this, watch your mind; it can get pretty crazy-making when you actually catch what's going on in there. No wonder the world is nuts, people are believing these thoughts are real.

The beauty of knowing such thoughts are there, is you get to catch them. Depending on how you're viewing them, (from your ego-mind or your God-mind), they can be annoying to the point of exhaustion. You may get down on yourself for believing you're not further along in your spiritual growth, another ego-ploy. Or, you can see them as incredibly ridiculous thoughts which have nothing to do with who you really are, and stop them in their tracks.

I've had plenty of entertaining thoughts. Whether I get a laugh out of it or roll my eyes with frustration, I simply hand it over to God, saying something like: "Look at these crazy thoughts *with* me. They're still trying to attack my peace of mind. I offer them to you because they don't belong here." Believe me, those thoughts may come even more often, once the ego realizes you're choosing against it. When that happens — take a breath and choose a few more seconds with God.

Another way to look at thoughts is they're showing you a belief you're subconsciously holding onto. Now you can become aware and release them. At one time, I'd find my mind wandering into a daydream of being in a loving relationship, only to have things not work out. Which felt awful, but familiar. That's a repetitive 'attack thought' against love. My daydreams were showing me how often the ego attempts to keep love away. This can be helpful when you take a look at what you're subconsciously believing, in order for such thoughts to be there in the first place.

There are many ways to look at these thoughts in order to shift your beliefs. Of course, being aware of an unproductive thought helps you get some distance from it. We tend to automatically believe the inner dialogue. Simply because it sounds convincing doesn't mean it's true, or that we have to engage it. We are so identified with our thoughts, we think they *are* us. Especially since the ego uses our own voice. (It's a very convincing tactic.)

We get upset with ourselves for the thoughts we think. But does it ever occur to us not to think those thoughts? A thought drops in and we feel some strange obligation to listen to it. We think: "Oh no, I had another fearful thought, it must be true. After all, I'm thinking it. It's mine. So I'll keep it." But it's not yours. It's got nothing to do with the real you.

Why do we feel such an obligation to a thought just because it landed in our field of awareness? If we don't like what we're thinking we get more and more upset, rather than stopping the cycle. The ego-mind is a closed loop, telling us: "I have a thought! It must be important. Let me suffer with this thought even more."

When do you have automatic judgments? That means opinions, beliefs, worries, even your values. All these hold a judgment. Don't judge yourself for judging, (another ego-tactic), just notice.

Make a list of judgments:

_____

_____

_____

Contemplation: What would you have to believe in order for these thoughts to show up? What would you have to believe, in order to do the things which don't work well for you? Write down some of the beliefs that provoke unhealthy thoughts and actions:

Example:

Judgment: Being upset by someone's success.

Belief: I don't deserve a good and easeful life.

_____

_____

_____

Once you discover a belief, you can become aware of who's talking, ego or God. Do you want to keep believing it, or is it time to let it go? Must this belief remain true? The ego may tell you some beliefs must remain true, and will provide you with plenty of evidence. But if you take those beliefs to God, you'll see whether they hold true in the face of who you really are.

If you hold destructive thoughts and beliefs, but ignore them by keeping busy, they're still in your subconscious mind running (or ruining) your life. Often we aren't even aware of all our beliefs, but instead we feel moody or turn judgmental. Here are four basic ego needs:

- need for approval;
- need for control;
- need for safety and security;
- need for separation.

All of these ego needs are setting us up for the ultimate need for separation from God. There's no reason you shouldn't have any of these met, but by whom? Have approval from yourself first. Have control, (of your state of mind), with the will of God, not the personal will which wants to control everything. Be safe and secure within yourself no matter what's happening. God doesn't *need* anything. So take 'need' out of the equation.

If you take a belief to the light of God, how does it change? That's why choosing for even one second is useful. Surrender the feeling over to your Higher Self. Once you do, though there's is no guarantee the situations in your life will change. The aim is not to make the dream exactly as you want it, but about waking up from the dream. What *is* guaranteed is you'll be more at peace no matter what, since you're elevating your perception.

CHAPTER 6

The "So What!" Mantra
Cutting Yourself And Others Some Slack

When you realize there is no lacking,
the whole world belongs to you.

- LAO TZU -

"WAIT! WHAT?" That was my response when I was in a
meditation workshop in India listening to a monk. She'd
been teaching for fifteen years. As she taught about the mind in
meditation, she remarked, "You know those times it takes about
twenty minutes to still your mind for meditation?" To be honest, I don't remember what else she said since I was shocked by
that alone. I remember thinking: *"If it takes **her** twenty minutes to
quiet the mind, I need to cut myself a lot of slack!"*

I decided not to be upset with the fact I have a human mind.
It's just doing what it does. I'd judged myself severely because I
had thoughts; that's like judging myself for breathing. What a
freeing realization. It gave me an awareness I wasn't my thoughts,
that thoughts just come.

But where do thoughts even come from? It's like they land

in our awareness while floating by. If certain thoughts resonate with us, we grab hold and make a story out of them. But there're many thoughts floating by we don't grab onto. We don't even notice them.

The thoughts we grab onto are the ones we identify with. It's a way for the ego-mind to keep its story alive. We live on a planet of stories. With eight billion people there are eight billion life stories. We continue to make up even more stories in the form of movies, books, theater, etc. So there's at least a gazillion stories here. Each thought we identify with has a story behind it. It's all a creation by the ego-mind.

This creation is the world of duality, right/wrong, good/evil. The stories are often about victory over evil-doers. Of course, who's evil is a matter of opinion. Every story has a winner and a loser, even the stories of our personal lives. In order to win, there's got to be something to win against. There's a lot of activity designed to keep us busy and distracted from peace.

The mind does what it does; thoughts come to us all the time. You're never going to micromanage your thoughts, nor would you want to, but you can be generally aware of your thoughts throughout the day. With this awareness, we can choose and let go, one second at a time. It doesn't mean you'll catch your mind all the time; just start noticing, *without judgment,* what's coming through.

The ego-mind can come up with some enticing stories to keep us stuck, even when we know we could choose otherwise. The ego will manipulate any thought to seem logical, normal. When that happens, we can forget to connect to our Higher Self.

Logic took over when my 85-year-old mother, who lived

by herself, left the gas on her stove, and a neighbor who happened to stop by immediately smelled it. She turned the stove off, opened the doors and windows and called me. I then called one of my brothers who lives near her and said: "Mom almost killed herself! If she wants to live alone then she has to settle for the refrigerator and microwave. Please go over there and shut off the gas." This seemed a reasonable strategy.

My brother answered, "No I'm not going to shut off the gas because she likes to cook."

"What do you mean?" I answered in shock. "She almost killed herself."

"But she didn't," he responded, "and I'm not taking away her one pleasure." What could I do? I'm over two thousand miles away in Arizona and he's right next door. As it turned out, none of my other siblings supported me.

I was fuming, and extremely worried. For the next three days my ego took me on a field trip. Not once did I remember to call on God for guidance or even to surrender for a moment. The fact is my ego's 'logic' made perfect sense to me: my brother should take care of my mom in the way I thought would keep her safe.

Here's the field trip the ego took me on: "I obviously care about my mother more than anyone else in the family. If she dies of asphyxiation, it's not my fault. Hang on, she'll be dead and I want to see her again. What if she dies in a fire? All those hours doing the rosary, and for what? She'll die in fear." The crescendo was: "You mean to tell me that I have to leave my business in Arizona to live with my physically healthy mother to protect her because no one else cares?!"

I took all these thoughts seriously; I was considering moving in with her. The ego-mind doesn't care if I'm happy; it likes drama. So now I was facing up-ending the life I'd built in Sedona. Then I had a realization: *oops, I forgot about the One-Second Cure.* I'd totally forgotten about God.

I sat on the couch, and said an embarrassed prayer: *"You can see I totally forgot about you, I was completely in the ego thought system for days. I just don't know what to do with my mom."* Then I got quiet. Finally. We all know answers to our prayers don't always arrive immediately, but this day one did. I received an inspired idea to put a camera on her stove. I said: *"God! God, that's brilliant!"*

Inspired ideas come from our Higher Self, while the ego-mind is usually planning on more misery. I called my brother, I expected push back, but he said: "Yes, great idea. Let's get three cameras." Since it was an inspired thought from Higher Self there was no pushback. Now, five years later, I check her stove daily. I can see if there are any concerns. My mother is still strong and living on her own at ninety.

Instead of getting down on myself for forgetting the One-Second Cure for three long days — during which time I'd tortured myself incessantly with fears — I simply said to my ego-mind, *"Good job, you had me for a long time there. Now I can choose otherwise".*

We can be so hard on ourselves. We make ourselves wrong all the time when we constantly follow false wisdom of the ego-mind. One result is the conviction we're never going to be happy. A constant barrage of negativity keeps us feeling bad while the ego-mind is delighted.

Catch your mind when you catch it, don't when you don't.
But when you do, implement the One-Second Cure.
Whatever you do, just don't judge yourself.

When a personal issue like my mother comes up, it can trig-ger deep emotional blocks to the presence of love. After all, she's my mom — of course we'd take care of her, but look where the conditioned mind took me with that story: days of suffering, making everyone else wrong and not even considering peace.

When such thoughts come up within you, be easy on your-self. Notice where you're not yet free from the conditioned mind, and maybe even get a little giggle out of it. You can laugh about believing the conditioned mind once again. That doesn't mean you ignore the feelings that come up, but you learn discernment between what is true, and what is false. This discernment allows feelings to be there without a story.

When I lived in the ashram in India I wrote to the Guru with some ego-rambling story about how it was hard to let go of my personal attachment to my body and appearance. I shared the whole story of wanting to let go of arrogance, and be more present. The letter went on, blah, blah, blah.

For me to write that letter took a lot of courage. I was hop-ing for a deep philosophical answer, confirming my devotion and sincere concerns about my spiritual path. A few days later one of her secretaries came to me with my answer. I was so excited in anticipation of receiving truth. The secretary said: "Your mes-sage was received, she wants you to lighten up!"

That was my answer, *to lighten up*? Yes, lighten up. Remem-ber "the tiny tick of time when the son of God remembered not to laugh."

Forgetting to laugh is what confirms our separated state. It's laughable because being separate isn't even a possibility. It's our *belief* making it seem real.

There *are* times to laugh at the ego-mind's intention to keep us from peace. I'm sure you've noticed the repetitive thoughts you've had for years still happening. Those thoughts may be worth laughing at, once you've called on Higher Self to look at them *with* you.

Some people could take this idea of remembering not to laugh to mean spiritually bypassing our issues; and take everything as a joke. Or they may think they shouldn't ever feel anything negative, so they focus on the positive without really doing their inner work. This represses the issues, while they remain active in the subconscious. When thoughts go unexamined, we keep them as beliefs.

There're plenty of times we may catch our ego and it doesn't seem like a laughing matter, such as my experience with my mom and the stove. When I did choose God after days of suffering, I didn't make myself wrong — I cut myself some slack. When issues come in any form, welcome them. As mentioned before, the Course teaches everyone is either calling for love or expressing love. This goes for our feelings as well. If we're rejecting or repressing them they're not feeling welcome, and they'll hang around hoping to be noticed eventually. Once you welcome these feelings, you're now allowing them without judgment. Once you welcome them, there's no resistance, and you can let them go.

The Course teaches we're never upset for the reason we

think; whatever bothers you can always be traced to belief in separation from God. We're upset because in those moments we're choosing the wrong teacher and we're not at peace. When something happens in our life, it's not so much what's happening but our response that matters. What comes up within us *is* our inner work. This doesn't mean you ignore what may need to be dealt with in your life. It means you look at the upset from the perspective of realizing we feel separate because we bought into the dream of separation. If family or friends upset us, we have a choice to get triggered and react, or sit with the feeling for a bit and choose otherwise. How we respond unfurls the energy we're putting out. When you're triggered, use the processes below.

Process: Remember all energies come up to be released.

When a difficult feeling comes up, allow and welcome it. If there's a situation upsetting you, allow the whole situation to just be there, without judgment.

1. Connect with Higher Self by getting back into the expansive experience from Chapter 4; or any way in which you feel connected. You may imagine the energy of your body inwardly expanding, making space for Higher Self/ God.

2. From this place: Ask Higher Self/God to look at the situation *with* you.

3. Now ask: Can I let go of this disturbance? Am I willing to let this go? Welcome whatever comes up. Keep your attention on your connection with peace as you look at this situation or feeling.

Once the ego's out of the way you'll come to a place of more presence and stillness. This is your real identity with Higher Self/God. From this perspective you can release the emotions or opinions you have about the story. Any response needed will come from this place of stillness. Responses don't always come immediately, but the intention to have a response has been set.

While doing this process, if resistance were to show up, welcome that as well. Ask the question: Can I let go of this resistance? Just be with the feeling without labeling or judging it. As soon as we label or judge, the ego-mind has stepped in to keep us from peace. We accept, not reject anything that comes up. God's energy is *inclusive of everything*.

Another process from *A Course in Miracles* is the Forgiveness Process. It's a foundational process and teaching of letting go into God.

Forgiveness Process:
1. I forgive the projection: (Getting clear what we're seeing is our own projected guilt).
2. I forgive myself for projecting this: (Seeing how we're identifying with this issue from the ego-mind, and thus believing the dream).
4. I call upon the Holy Spirit/Higher Self for correction. (The correction is returning our attention to God after we have yet again fallen under the spell of the dream).

It's not always necessary to find the seed cause of our issues. Sometimes people seek answers from past life regression or through therapy while reviewing family of origin issues from this lifetime. For some people it can be useful to understand situations which helps them let go. But what if you can't find the reason something is happening? Ultimately it's all just energy coming up to be released. We can never really know on the level of our dream why anything's happening. The idea of looking for the seed cause can keep us in seeking mode or always looking for something to heal. This can keep us really busy 'fixing' our lives, and not letting go of the story. It's about bringing our darkness to Higher Self/God, not fixing everything.

Looking for answers in the story of our lives comes from the mistaken belief the world of the ego-mind *is* the real world. That said, it can be useful to contemplate our patterns and notice what we're holding onto. But if you can't find the issue, that's okay. It's just not necessary. So when an emotion or issue comes up, this is the time to sit and remove ourselves from the story and call on Higher Self/God.

We've fallen into Maya, or illusion, again. That's ok. Notice without judgment you stepped back in the story. As soon as you notice you're back in the story, you're actually out of the story. You're now aware. Once you're out, you're out. Extend the time out as much as you can. When you step out, it doesn't mean you may not still feel uncomfortable. Once you do the processes and release, you'll feel more peaceful or centered within yourself.

Cutting yourself and others some slack

We've often heard the idea we should love ourselves more. With everything that can come up how do you do that? Especially if we tend to get down on ourselves.

The best way to love yourself is to cut yourself some slack.

We're so hard on ourselves. I want to offer you a mantra to use whenever you feel down on yourself for not being perfect, or for having negative thoughts or experiences. We so easily get caught up in the conditioned mind again and again.

Are you ready for your new mantra?

It's what I call the "So What!" mantra. For instance: You've said something that didn't come out right, and you're worried people will be upset with you…

"So What!"

You had negative thoughts toward someone all day and you preferred to hang onto it instead of using the One Second Cure…

"So What!"

Maybe you didn't send love or call on Higher Self, not even once. You may hear a voice in your head say: "You're such a failure, you can't even take a second to send a blessing." Or: "This is too hard, I can't do this. This is stupid anyway." When you catch this kind of self talk, stop. Who's talking?

"So What!"

Congratulations! You've caught the ego doing its thing. That's what I call success. Even if you're not feeling great about it, the fact is when you're observing and noticing what's happening, you're no longer with the ego in those moments.

By the way, who says that catching the ego has to happen in real time anyway? The ego does, then you can feel like a failure. But you can get familiar with its games. At the end of the day when you realize you just threw hostile darts at someone all day, simply thank the ego-mind for reminding you. Remember to welcome and accept whatever feelings come up.

Start being kind to yourself when you fall into the conditioned mind's arena: "So What!"

Remember, I was in fear, anger and confusion about my brother for days for not shutting off my mother's gas stove. When I finally caught the ego-mind, I was able to look at the issue with God. Until then I went on a field trip to hell in my head. We've been there before and we'll do it again... until we don't. "So What!"

However, saying the "So What!" mantra by itself without switching your thoughts to right-minded thinking is just repressing your issues. Looking at what's upsetting you with your right-minded thoughts is what changes your perception. While you are cutting yourself some slack, cut others some slack too.

CHAPTER 7

If They Coulda Done Better,
They Woulda Done Better...

Losing an illusion makes you wiser than finding a truth.
- LUDWIG BÖRNE -

ONE WAY to cut others some slack is simply not to judge them. To forgive anyone for the things you think they've done can be too difficult, especially if it feels like forgiveness means you're condoning someone's behavior. I've heard people say, "Oh, I've definitely forgiven them," as their voice gets higher-pitched and their body tenses up. You've taken the higher road, and forgiven them for what you think they've done.

This is the kind of forgiveness the *Song of Prayer* addition to the Course calls "forgiveness to destroy." It's forgiveness from the ego's point of view: excusing someone for what you think they did in the dream. This keeps both of you trapped in the world of illusion, ensuring your separateness. There's always a one-upmanship with the ego's form of forgiveness: *I'm better than that person because I forgave them.*

True forgiveness is release from believing in the illusions

ego creates. When you attempt to forgive an illusion you're making that particular illusion real — trapping yourself. Instead, you acknowledge we're all dreaming. Since the dream only reflects back to us what the mind thinks, this gives you the opportunity to see what's within you, which keeps you tied to the ego's dream.

"Forgiveness recognizes that what you thought your brother did to you has not occurred. ...Forgiveness merely sees its falsity, and therefore lets it go. What then is free to take its place is now the Will of God." [1]

The will of God is always available to you in the real world as God created it — the world of inner peace — and not the world of chaos and confusion the ego created. When you notice you are judging someone, there's a few ways to look at this.

First, on a practical level (in the level of the dream), repressing something isn't forgiveness. Repressing means burying the issues deep in your psyche. This isn't freedom, nor will it lead to inner peace. You might realize the person in question wasn't able to make a better choice, or they would've. Somehow you expected that person to be more evolved than they are (in your opinion of course), and you get really upset when you feel they should have acted differently.

But they *didn't* act differently. So, any resentment, anger, or judgment means you're not accepting reality as it is, which will only upset you. You could understand they're on their own journey, and your judgments won't change that.

If you were raised in a Judeo-Christian religion you've heard: "Forgive them, for they know not what they do." In reality that's true; if they could do better, they would do better. So it's a matter of accepting that fact and blessing them on their journey, meanwhile freeing yourself of ideas and concepts of how things 'should be'. Anything else is fighting with a dream, literally. This acceptance is a step out of the dream, toward inner peace and the truth of who you are. So your judgment on how much further along someone else 'should be' on their journey isn't reality.

Maybe there's someone in your life you're holding a resentment toward, or blaming for something, and you're having a hard time letting go.

Bring someone to mind you're holding a grievance about, or someone who triggers you. **For starters, try not to choose your most difficult person(s).** But if you do, this can be very healing. If you feel there's no one in your life who bothers you, then who triggers you, or annoys you? Who do you wish would act differently, or is there a situation you want to be different than it is. I always love it when someone tells me no one triggers them, but when I mention any political figure they don't appreciate, they automatically have something to work with.

MAKE A "FORGIVENESS" LIST

It can be people who have really hurt you, or people who just bug you — include friends, family, politicians, et al.

_____

_____

_____

Step back and observe each of these people. Notice how you expect them to be other than how they are. To really accept them is to accept the fact they actually can't be any other way *at* *this moment.* The way we hold them in our mind ensures they'll show up as we expect. It's not up to us to try and change people; you want them to be different so *you* can be at ease. I used to try and plant a seed of change in my brother and if that didn't work, then I'd try screaming at him, (as if that helped anything). Ultimately I realized I wanted him to be different so I could be happy. I couldn't stand the conflict he created (though it was actually me creating the conflict). It was like me telling a tree to uproot and move over six feet since the sun was better in the other spot. Well, that ain't gonna happen, and neither is me trying to move a person off their belief system until they are ready.

I was so insistent that he be different, every time I saw him I would throw hate bombs at him, which cocooned him in the energy of hate. He wouldn't disappoint, he always showed up exactly as I expected. He enraged me. The more I decided to send loving intentions at him, he showed up softer, nicer more approachable. He hasn't changed his belief system, he's still the same person. I now accept him as he is. If I get triggered, and I still can, I do the inner work needed for *me* to be free.

It finally occurred to me maybe just letting him be as he is, would actually create more peace. People change when they've had enough of themselves, not when we've had enough of them. People have to want things to be different themselves to finally reach out to a higher power. Everyone finally calls for true help in their own timing. In the meantime, if I'm triggered by them, it's my stuff I've got to look at. **Besides, I don't have to hang out with anyone who upsets me. My upset is just not their fault.**

Is it possible to see others mired in the ego-mind, (as we're all conditioned to be), and to view them as someone calling out for love? Can we have compassion for them? If not, that's okay, but would you want to *be* them? The answer is always no. Can you then have compassion for the fact they have to be themselves, even with all their belief in suffering? They don't know how not to be them. Their life experiences have led them to be the way they are. Whether you think so or not, they're working their way through life the best they can.

As you choose God, pick a person from your list. Do they still bug you? The one thing I can guarantee you, is God won't be agreeing with you: *"Yup, you're right! There's been a mistake with that person. I get it, they're annoying as hell!"* But God *could* be saying: "Have you *looked* around this planet? It's crazy. *I need more representation here. Could you do me a favor and send this person just one second of love or compassion from your Higher Self to their Higher Self? After all, this person is on their way back home too."* They're calling out for love, and in that moment you can be '*God's representative*' (seeing from a higher perspective) and extend love. Just for a second. As you look at this person from *above the battleground*, you can easily let them be as they are, knowing they too are believing they're separate from God. We're all in the same story.

We all remember our home in God. But we each have to choose to make that connection. Until we choose differently we're listening to the ego voice as our inner teacher. Nobody's yet succeeded in insisting someone think differently. It's up to us to experience our life from the Higher Self, and let that emanate into the world. If this exercise is difficult right now, then add: "I'm *willing* to let this go, I'm *willing* to see this differently."

This would be a great time to use the forgiveness process from Chapter 6:
I forgive the projection,
I forgive myself for projecting it.
And I call upon Higher Self for correction (shifting our attention to God).

Again, the correction is that one second we remember to return our attention to God after we've yet again fallen under the spell of the dream. I love this process because it provides the perspective that we're buying into a dream which emanates from us, and we can change our perception of the dream.

My father was someone I loved to hate for decades, for good reason. He was really wounded as a child and his trauma translated into his parenting. As he was the priest of our church all I could see was his hypocrisy. At least that was my perception. He loved to wear his priest collar whenever he would go out, and I felt he was using his clothing to get respect in the community. In my opinion, he didn't deserve it.

Little did I know at that time, he was a mirror for my beliefs, showing me my own hypocrisy. Even though I didn't appreciate him wearing his priest collar in public, I definitely wanted him to wear it when I brought him to meet my Guru near my home town of Syracuse. When my Guru saw a priest at the ashram, she asked one of her staff to bring him to her. Turns out that collar was handy after all! We sat with her for two hours while people gathered around us on the lawn. It was a wonderful evening of conversation and jokes. I was so happy to sit in her presence.

Even so, it didn't take long for her to notice the tension

between my father and me. I couldn't hide the fact I didn't like sitting close to him. He crossed a boundary by reaching over and holding my hand. Every cell in my body screamed. In front of the Guru I couldn't cause a scene as I normally would. So I waited a few seconds and removed his hand from mine. Two minutes later he did it again. This time I took his hand, leaned over to him and said under my breath, "You're pushing your limits." You didn't have to be an enlightened being to see the problem between us, even if I thought whispering would help.

As it happened, my father loved being with the Guru. There was a lot of playful interaction between them. After, he would come to the ashram often throughout the summer. He was treated like a VIP in the ashram and the staff always took care of his needs, making sure he was seated near the Guru when he was around. Throughout the summer, every time I'd bump into the Guru in the ashram, she'd say to the people around her, "Did you know her father's a priest?" This happened several times, and I loved getting attention from her.

That winter I went to India to live in the ashram there. I was a nurse in the medical clinic. I went up with the clinic staff to greet the Guru for Christmas. I was happy to have been elected by the group to present her with our Christmas gift. As I handed her the gift on behalf of our staff, she said to everyone, "Did you know her father's a priest?"

There it was again. I had to admit to myself my father really was a priest. Despite my disdainful opinion of him, I was being asked to look beyond the ego-mind and see my father from God's point of view. I could stay in my ego-mind and suffer, or I could see him as another person working his way out of the dream and into truth.

I wrote her a note saying: "I get it, my father *really is* a priest." The answer from her secretary was simply, "Very good." She never mentioned it again.

As I continued doing my inner work and lived more from my heart, I realized I wouldn't have wanted to be him. I wouldn't have wanted his life experiences; they had left him traumatically damaged and mentally off (just enough to drive his family crazy). When I realized I wouldn't want to be him, he went from being my nemesis to someone who did the best job he could raising us. He didn't have any of the resources we have today. He didn't have the books, or coaches, or YouTube teachers. He had nothing but his conditioning.

So if I wouldn't want to be him, could I have compassion for the fact that *he* had to be him? Yes, I could do that. When we really step into someone else's experience the only truthful response is compassion. My father was always calling out for love, as is everyone who is wounded in some way and thus identified with the ego-mind. In my conflicts with him, I also was calling out for love.

Everyone is either calling out for love
or expressing love.

It's not just others we judge; we can be insanely hard on ourselves. In my opinion, I've done some pretty stupid and embarrassing things. I can hear myself say, "I should've known better!" Yes, but obviously I didn't. That is, I was making myself wrong for being on a learning curve. I looked back into my life and saw there was no other way for me to have acted in those moments, given my life experience.

Once I saw the issue, I had a choice to let it go. We tend to hold ourselves up to a very high standard. Just being willing to forgive yourself is huge. To forgive yourself is to accept where you'd been at any moment in your life, and acknowledge that you've learned from it.

In forgiving yourself you're letting go of who you are not — this character in the dream — and joining with God.

The ego-mind never has any intention of letting go, which is why stepping into your Higher Self is your ticket to freedom.

Make another list:

Things you still regret you did, or didn't do, that you're not proud of:

_____

_____

_____

1) For each item, write down how you see it from the ego's point of view.

Get a separate piece of paper and just let it all out. Go on for pages if you need to about everything you think should have been different; how embarrassed you still are; and how you should have known better. Write down what you think your life could have been like if you'd only done things differently.

2) When you've finished, imagine you're seeing this same situation from God's point of view. Now write down everything that comes from connecting to your Higher Self. *If there's any judgment at all, you're still in the ego.* Write down everything your Higher Self has to say. Notice the compassion and the acceptance. Don't forget to breathe!

Which inner teacher do you want to be listening to? Which one wants to keep you stuck and suffering, and which one is leading you to wake up from the dream?

Observe the insistence of the ego-mind to keep you feeling unhappy, and how easily we tend to accept that decision — until now.

We're forgiving ourselves for what we haven't really done. We forgive ourselves for buying into the dream yet again. You don't wake up in the morning and make yourself wrong for dreaming a dream you had at night. You may glean some insight from it, and journal about it. It's the same thing with our 'waking' dream. Instead of making yourself wrong, take what you need to continue waking up from this experience.

CHAPTER 8

The World Isn't Your Fault,
But You're Involved

Do your little bit of good where you are; it's those
little bits of good put together that overwhelm the world.
- DESMOND TUTU -

T HE TERM "butterfly effect" was coined in the 1960's by Edward Lorenz, a meteorology professor at the Massachu-setts Institute of Technology, who was studying weather pat-terns. The idea was that any small change in the weather system can have enormous consequences. Just the flapping of a but-terfly's wings could contribute to a cyclone somewhere else on the planet.

At the time, weather statisticians thought you should be able to predict future weather based on looking at historical records. Running a computer program to test various weather simulations, Lorenz discovered rounding off one variable from .506127 to .506 dramatically changed the two months of weath-er predictions in this simulation.* That's a small variation, with such different effects, one a storm, and one calm. There are too many variables to actually say a butterfly's wings contribute to a cyclone.

However this idea of the subtle flapping of the butterfly's wings became a general phrase used to indicate any small changes could possibly have greater consequences. It goes right along with System Theory, which states any change, positive or negative, affects the whole system.

This idea goes beyond the weather. When I first learned about the Butterfly Effect, I was a raging maniac. I just didn't know it. I complained a lot, I often experienced road rage, and I must have loved fighting with my brother, because I did it well. (The man is 6'2" with muscles, you'd think I'd know better.) Nothing felt right in my world. But I could justify all my behavior, so of course I believed I was right and everyone else was wrong.

Since the idea that any change in the system could affect the entire system, I had to consider what I was doing. My merest movements on this planet are part of a larger system. That includes walking to my car, waving at a friend, acting-out with road rage, or screaming at anything that moved.

Now what happens when some eight billion people act from their ego-minds, projecting their hatreds and fears out into the world? What happens, is what we have, a world filled with division, hatred, war, homelessness, disease... the list goes on.

Given even small variances can cause significantly different outcomes, imagine if we were just a little kinder to each other. Everything would be completely different. We're all contributing collectively. What we do matters to the whole, spiritually speaking, because we are literally all one.

The realization that we are all one struck me one day years ago when I was working as a registered nurse in a very busy medical center. The caseload was too much for one nurse. I had five patients that day, all of them quite ill. Two patients were sick enough to be in the Intensive Care Unit, and I was trying to get them there.

There were pages of orders to get started, and in front of me were the family members of these patients, wanting my attention. If I could've walked away at that moment without being arrested for patient abandonment, I would've. As I was feeling this overwhelming need to scream, I turned my attention to one of the family members. My consciousness left this 'normal' level of awareness and went to a moment of pure oneness.

Everything around me became one vibrant energy. When I looked at the person who a second ago I felt overwhelmed by, now crying about their family member, I realized I was looking at myself. Literally myself. I looked around, everything which had been separate a second ago was now all an alive energy of oneness. Every person *was* me, every object, the same energy.

This insight lasted only a moment, long enough for me to realize things aren't as they seem. I had a glimpse of the real world. Soon the veil of our 'normal' reality fell around me again, and I was back in the world of separation — a world designed to veil the truth from us. It's not that the world had changed; I'd seen it differently.

Our belief in the dream of separateness keeps us firmly asleep. I'd gotten a glimpse. Why then? Because sometimes when things get so intense, there's nowhere to go but inside. But it doesn't have to be that way. There's a saying, in order to obtain enlightenment you have to want God as much as a drowning man wants air. I don't believe that at all. Though there has to be some disillusionment about the world and our investment in it. There's a dawning on us that there has to be another way.

When you change your perception from within, you change your world. Practice seeing the world with oneness; let the world do what it does. It's been doing it all this time anyway, with or without your approval. Once you pick a side on any issue, or judge anything, you're in the dream again. Every unexamined thought, every projected hatred or self-righteous idea helps create our perception of the conflicted world we see at any given moment. Remember there's good here too; that's duality. Thoughts create our mixed reality. We may not always change the outer world when we change our thoughts, but we can change our perception of the world, cultivating inner peace. A much more useful experience to share.

The Course says: "There is no world apart from what you wish, and therein lies your ultimate release. Change your mind on what you want to see, and the world must change accordingly. Ideas leave not their source." [1]

This means if you constantly engage in wrong-minded thoughts you'll unfurl a reality determined by the ego-mind's point of view, replete with judgment and fear. When you choose right-minded thoughts, you'll experience more peace and joy in your life, no matter the outside events. The two thought systems take you in completely opposite directions. It's not that outer events will change, (though it's possible) it's about looking without judgment, in observer mode.

This isn't about changing over to positive thinking; it's about our misidentification with the ego-minded thoughts we believe. Thinking more positive thoughts is definitely a better choice and feels a lot better. However it's realizing we're in a dream so we can finally awaken from it. "Every thought you have contributes to truth or to illusion." [2]

The ego is 'fight' energy; it fights to be right. It'll even die to be right. Whenever we scream at the television, that contributes to us staying in the belief of the dream world. The same energy also contributes to the whole. That's what we're sharing and teaching others. We teach by demonstration. We've all heard, teach by example. I don't get to scream at someone in righteous indignation and then decide where the energy goes. You don't get to choose where that energy goes. It goes into the collective, joining other energies like itself. It has an impact on others and reinforces our own ego-minded perception.

With all this being said, in a way, we've all contributed to the chaos on the planet. It's not our fault, yet collectively we *are* involved. The 'outer world' is an outward expression of our inner collective battle. We've also all contributed to all the great things on the planet, that's duality. As we awaken from the dream, we then get to choose whether to continue to make the world real by projecting our fears onto it. However, as we allow and observe the world without our projections we're no longer contributing, but awakening.

Carl Jung wrote: "A group experience takes place on a lower level of consciousness than the experience of an individual. This is due to the fact that, when many people gather together to share one common emotion, the total psyche emerging from the group is below the level of the individual psyche. If it is a very large group, the collective psyche will be more like the psyche of an animal, which is the reason why the ethical attitude of large organizations is always doubtful. The psychology of a large crowd inevitably sinks to the level of mob psychology. If, therefore, I have a so-called collective experience as a member of a group, it takes place on a lower level of consciousness than if I had the experience by myself alone."

The group mind is the lowest form of consciousness. Look at the world, not just now, but in our history of group-think. When people think with the group-mind, it's all collective thoughts with no personal responsibility. That's why we've all heard the defenses made after war crimes. They were only following orders. There's no one there to critically think differently from the group mind.

Thankfully, we'll *all* wake up from the collective ego-mind thought system. Somewhere along the way I heard this amazing saying, I wish I could remember where: "We are all asleep together on this planet. But we're waking up like popcorn." Such a great analogy since it presupposes we'll all awaken.

What kind of thoughts I contribute to the group collective is my decision. As we learn to forgive the idea of separation, one second at a time, we can see the world and the people in it trying to fight their way out of a small box called the ego-mind. I remember when I first started being aware of my beliefs, I felt as if I were living in a very small box. I was constantly bumping into self-imposed limitations. (I just didn't know at the time they were self-imposed.) Later, as I continued doing my inner work and shifting some beliefs, I stood in the middle of my living room and complained out loud: "I'm just living in a larger box!" At some point we realize there's no need to fight or even fix things, there's just letting go. There are no boxes, it's allowing everything without judgment.

The poet-saint Rumi said:
"Out beyond ideas of wrongdoing
and rightdoing there is a field.
I'll meet you there."

Am I listening to Higher Self, or ego as my inner teacher? I know I'm likely to continue thinking from the ego-mind, (until I don't). How could I not after so many lifetimes of conditioning? Again, it's always a one second choice, catching myself in the wrong mind, then choosing otherwise.

ACIM says "Anger is never justified." It doesn't mean you won't feel anger, but it's not justified. People do what they do, and we get triggered. It's pretty funny once you see what's happening. Again we want others to act differently so *we* can be happy. The outside world isn't going to change enough to make anyone happy; where would we start? Especially with eight billion people involved. And what's the right way to change, according to whom?

When you blame others, the 'outside' world is now your reality, not your inner world. There's no peace in the outer world. Someone or something will disappoint you, hurt you, leave you. Nevertheless you can and will have peace even while living in this world, no matter what's happening.

Even after I'd been meditating for twelve years, I'd not yet integrated the higher teachings to which I was exposed. I meditated in the morning, and I screamed at cars in the afternoon. I was still proficient at road rage — actually, any kind of rage, period. Every time a car cut me off, I'd scream, shout and take it as a personal affront. It's funny now to see I took it personally. For those of us who may still suffer from road rage, self righteous indignation and rage are seemingly normal reactions from the ego-mind's point of view. Yet that's another story to keep us stuck. The ego thrives on drama so it's going to amp up the drama game. It's a great way to keep us in the story it's created, and far from peace.

I really wanted to change my tactics. What I was doing wasn't working. Luckily an inspired solution came to mind. I realized I could choose differently — by sending a blessing to the cars instead. What a great idea. I decided to choose God. As another car cut me off I put my hand out to extend a blessing and said these words aloud: "I'm with you God, I choose you." I raised my hand to extend the blessing. Here's how the blessing came out instead.

"Screw you! I'm not gonna bless you, you almost killed me!"

Not exactly what I intended my blessing to sound like. I remember looking down at my body filled with rage, and thinking; how am I supposed to send a blessing to that person when I'm consumed with adrenaline? I realized I was justifying my angry response. Remember, anger is never justified. I can feel it and release it. But how I feel is never that other person's fault.

What I do with rage is up to me. I can dump it onto the world, continuing to make the world seem real, and contribute to the collective insanity. Or I can let go of the dream world (the situation) by choosing peace. Besides, I have no idea how many lifetimes I've been carrying this rage with me. If other lifetimes are required, I'd prefer not to take it with me, yet again.

After several failed attempts at sending a blessing, (the ego doesn't want to let go), a car sped by me and cut me off. I raised my hand and said: "Be careful, you're not driving safely." That was it, a simple act of kindness. I didn't call on Archangel Michael or put white light around the car. That wasn't even possible for me back then. I wasn't very loving. However, I could offer a simple act of kindness. There wasn't any sarcasm, and when I checked my body, there wasn't any adrenaline. There was just an extension of kindness. What struck me most is I genuinely meant it. If you can do it once, you can do it again. You've broken through a little bit more of the illusory ego-mind.

One of the highest tenets of Buddhism is loving kindness, not toward the people you already like, (that's easy), but toward the people you have strong opinions about and judge. The Dalai Lama told a story about when the Chinese took over Tibet and murdered thousands of people, as well as imprisoning many monks. After twenty years a jailed monk escaped and he found his way to India where the Dalai Lama was living. His Holiness was curious and wondered if this monk was ever in danger. He admitted he meant physical danger. The monk replied that he'd been in danger twice. The Dalai Lama asked, "What happened?" And the monk said, "I almost lost my compassion twice."

If anyone were to lose their compassion it should've been this monk. To stay with the decision for Higher Self in these extreme situations is incredible. If he could do that, then I could start by sending kindness to passing cars, or people I've held resentments toward.

As I extended kindness to the cars cutting me off, I felt better. I felt as if I was doing something positive for the planet. I was definitely doing something positive for myself as I was more calm and centered, and I wasn't sending negative energy out into the world. (At least while I was in my car.)

I started to look forward to the next car cutting me off, since I was now ready to extend kindness to them. I saw this as my new job. Remarkably enough the energy around me changed. After about seven months of extending kindness, cars stopped cutting me off. Same highway, same time of day — nothing had changed except me.

I remember feeling disappointed because I liked my new job of sending kindness to cars. I asked what happened. The response was: The outside world wasn't happening *to* me, it was happening *by* me. When I changed myself, my experience changed.

Now the fact is, the outside world can change, and it very well may not. I had no expectations the cars would stop cutting me off. My experience changed. Even if the cars never stopped, I was content to extend kindness forever. Each time I blessed a car it was one second more I was choosing God. Those seconds add up.

The response continued: if I liked my new job of blessing cars so much, I should take this idea to work. I was still working as a registered nurse, and I complained constantly. I can scream alone in my car all I want, but the only person to see me act like a fool is me. If I screamed at people at work I'd get fired. Complaining is just socialized rage, and I did it well.

There was a doctor who I felt was really negative. (Talk

about projection.) I spent a decade avoiding her, or rolling my eyes every time I saw her. I'd throw her hateful thoughts several times a day. When the message came to take this idea to work, in my mind she became the next passing car. Over many months of silently sending her love instead, she finally sat next to me one day and started chatting. Wow. We became friendly at work for the rest of my employment there. A ten-year resentment I'd held toward her was now over.

Nothing's right from the ego's point of view. The ego never accepts what's happening about anything. Feeling aggrieved is how the ego keeps us aligned with itself. Complaints are constant because only the ego knows how to run the world. Anger flares up when opinions face opposition, which happens most of the time. Eight billion egos wanting to run the world from their point of view — no wonder there are constant wars.

The fact is the ego-mind loves to make up stories which aren't true. My resentment toward the busy doctor may have started when she ignored me one morning after I said hello. Maybe she didn't even hear me. Let's be honest, she's a very busy, focused oncologist. The ego made up a story about how wronged I was, then persuaded me to see her as a villain for years. The ego would rant: *"Who does she think she is? I can't believe how rude she is. I'm not talking to her, I'll ask the charge nurse to interpret her illegible doctor's handwriting. I'm not getting near her. She's not even approachable."* This is what the ego does, creating fictions from little or no evidence.

How many misunderstandings have you experienced which simply vanished when looking at things differently? These really aren't misunderstandings; they're ego-ploys to keep you aligned with it. We can fall into these stories so easily. How many people die with resentments, holding onto false stories which could be cleared up if they'd stepped out of the ego-mind. It takes a second to enter your heart and see the situation from Higher Self's perspective. That's the only sure path to understanding, forgiveness, and the discovery of solutions otherwise unknown.

When someone really bugs you, thank them for showing you where you still have work to do.

We don't have to do big things to contribute to peace on the planet. In *The Last Hours of Ancient Sunlight,* Thom Hartmann wrote that there are many simple things we can do to make a difference in the world. One example is seeing a worm stuck in a puddle after a rainstorm, and taking the time to put the worm back on the grass. This seemingly unimportant act of kindness takes seconds, and it sends out loving vibrations for everyone. This example isn't meant to make the dream world real, it's about choosing Higher Self at any given moment. If I'm called to help a worm then I can. This sets a loving vibration in me. And sends out a loving vibration for all people who still believe in the dream.

Shortly after I read Hartman's book, I was walking to work after a rainstorm and came across a worm in a puddle. Was this a pop quiz? I took a second or two to get the worm out of the puddle and put it on the grass. Really it took me about 3-4 long minutes with a stick to get it out of the puddle. I don't like touching worms. But I did it!

Little things do matter. I remember driving in my car when a construction worker smiled at me. That was it, just a smile. What I felt was a genuine connection. I felt an immediate shift in my energy. In that moment I realized we're literally transmitting energy. What we put out there matters. The Butterfly Effect can be activated with just a smile.

EXERCISE:

List ways you are unintentionally contributing to the chaos in the world. Include familiar complaints. Or times you aren't accepting what's happening without judgment.

_____

_____

_____

Now, do one or any of the forgiveness processes we've reviewed. Be aware of which mind you're listening to. Who's talking? Are you willing to let this go? Can you let this go? Will you let this go? Sit with the feelings and offer them to Higher Self. Again we're never upset for the reasons we think. Ultimately we're upset because we're not at peace in any given moment.

In countless small ways, one second at a time, we can begin to choose our Higher Self over our conditioned mind. Let's say you take the opportunity to send a loving thought to someone you usually throw poisonous darts at. If you can choose your Higher Self at that moment, then, you're *not* "fixing a habit" — you've fundamentally changed your entire perception. That's one second of kindness more than yesterday. Again, you're not being kind to their ego, you're seeing there *is* no separation. You're being kind to yourself.

How we treat others is how we feel about ourselves. We

can continue filling ourselves with anger at everything that happens and project that into the world, or we can choose to forgive the dream. The choice is ours to make, second by second.

Here's the best part: whenever you don't make new choices, it's not right or wrong, or good or bad. It's just a matter of how long you want to keep feeling angry or depressed about the world, the people in it, and yourself. How long do you want to hold onto a perception which keeps you unhappy? You don't have to be perfect to let things go. There just has to be a little willingness.

> **You don't have to be perfect.**
> **You just have to be willing.**

---

* "What Is the Butterfly Effect and How Do We Misunderstand It?" by Nathan Chandler (*howstuffworks.com*, updated 6/9/23).

CHAPTER 9

Still Clueless

In the midst of movement and chaos,
keep stillness inside you.
- ALAN WATTS -

THREE BUNK BEDS. Six women. One bathroom. I never thought I'd find myself living in such close proximity to so many people. I was on staff in the ashram and that was our living arrangement. We were rarely in our rooms as the ashram schedule kept us very busy with meditation, chanting, and work as well. There were also courses and talks to attend. It was a very nurturing experience; I felt completely at home.

When I lived in the ashram I'd occasionally see someone crying as they walked down the hall. I knew something was up — but at age 36, four years into my ashram experience, I hadn't yet become fully aware of the ego's influence on my life.

One summer day I was in my room with only one other roommate, who was weeping. I knew enough to give her privacy and yet I felt for her. So I asked, "Is everything okay?" She responded, "Yeah, I just have issues." You'd think I'd have known what that meant, but I hadn't even begun to work on myself.

I remember thinking: What does she mean 'issues'? What are issues?

As I thought about that, I had an insight, (more like a delusion), and said out loud to myself: "Gee… I'm either very pure and spiritually advanced (meaning I have no issues), or I'm seriously blocked." I can't believe I actually said that out loud. What an invitation to the universe to show me how blocked I was.

I thought I'd come to terms with all my childhood traumas because I'd simply acknowledged them. It never occurred to me I'd repressed my feelings. I was about to find out I was sitting on a ton of unconscious issues.

For starters, I was about to get married for all the wrong reasons. One of the reasons was being 36 and still single, (as if that's a good reason). I felt since I was the last single sibling in my family, it was time to get married. This feeling was intensified by having lived in the ashram for four years, totally celibate. Somehow it never occurred to me to just to date this guy.

I met my soon-to-be husband in the ashram in India. He was from California and was just my type: dysfunctional. Cute, though. That seemed to be my entire criteria, time to get married, and a cute guy. My perfect match. I was working as an R.N. in the ashram clinic, helping get staff members in for their checkups. It was a hot Indian day and we were set up outside. I had no interest in anything except for meditation, being quiet and yoga. I was definitely not interested in men; only God.

When he walked in for his check-up, everything stopped. All my attention riveted on him (God who?). It was the perfect meeting of two people who had tons of inner work to do. He was married already (of course he was), but unhappily he said (now there's a line), thinking about getting a divorce from his second wife (run, red flag! I'd be wife number 3!) who was in America. Once we met, the divorce proceedings began.

Once I agreed to get married, all kinds of uncomfortable feelings arose. I didn't know why I felt so unsure of my decision. So, for the first time in my life I started to contemplate what was prompting my feelings. I progressed rapidly from not knowing what an issue was, to writing out page after page of them. Belief after belief came out — about men, about my worthiness, my lovability, my feelings of lacking safety and security. My need to be approved of, my lack of boundaries. Then there were beliefs about money, about family. The list went on forever. I was a total mess.

In my head I went from wrongfully imagining I was very spiritually advanced, to the realization I wasn't as cool as I'd imagined. And now I'd agreed to marry this man. I was having feelings of impending doom; I didn't yet have enough inner strength to make a wise decision for myself. The wall of doom would settle down around me with a palpable, paralyzing thickness. There was no light inside its confines. I felt like the witch in the Wizard of Oz about to have a house drop on her. Frankly that would have been a relief.

I needed help. All this need for inner work was new to me and I wasn't doing well. I decided to make an appointment with a psychologist who was also staying at the ashram. He was a native of India but now living in America.

I told him how conflicted I was about getting married, that I didn't know my fiancé well enough yet, so perhaps I should wait. I explained I didn't yet trust my own guidance. His response: "Well, people in India have arranged marriages all the time. Couples don't know each other well and it works." I'm thinking: "Well I'm not in India, I'm an American girl, from New York, by the way." When I asked, "What if it's a mistake?" he answered, "Well, you won't know, but it's ok. If you make a mistake you can always divorce." He added, "Maybe you're just experiencing pre-marital jitters."

Seriously? Even I knew this wasn't sound advice. I needed to talk with someone who really could help, obviously we had a cultural difference. So I made an appointment with a psychiatrist, also at the ashram, who was from England. After I outlined my misgivings about marriage, he said, "Well, people in India have arranged marriages and they don't know each other well. It can work."

What?! Was there a glitch in the Matrix?

When I told him I feared making a serious mistake, he offered, "Well, you don't know, it's okay to make a mistake, you can always get a divorce. Maybe it's just pre-marital jitters." I was flabbergasted; reaching out for sound advice from professionals had netted me exactly the same advice twice, verbatim. What were the odds of that? In my case 100% because it happened.

I'd no idea what to do except keep moving forward. I also was accepting my 'pre-marital jitters' which still felt like impending doom. It would be a while before I realized at this point in my life I was incapable of saying 'no' on my own behalf. Here's a clue for anyone similarly confused: if there's any doubt, wait. A true yes is joyful and full hearted, knowing it's right to move forward. Mired in the ego's thought system, the obvious can seem obscure.

There are so many of us who have had lives without much

joy. The model for joy wasn't there. If we don't have good boundaries preserving a strong sense of self-worth, there's no way a healthy choice can be made.

Once married, we drove across the country visiting places in the Southwest, including the Grand Canyon. I was out of my body the entire time, freaking out and not knowing what to do. I was a ball of anxiety and doom, spending a lot of time lying down, rocking back and forth in the fetal position whenever I could be alone.

Usually people need a reservation well in advance to take a donkey ride down to the bottom of the Grand Canyon. But 'luckily' for us, we easily reserved a trek on short notice. The Grand Canyon is dry, vast, deep; about how I felt. There was a huge hole in me. I was mechanically getting around, but I don't think I was in my body at all.

There were about fifteen people going down the Canyon that day, and guides brought each of us our donkey for an introduction. In the ashram I'd learned the Sanskrit word 'judd', meaning spiritually dense — so dense even God can't get in. Some of us would tease each other about being judd.

The guide came up to me with my donkey, and said, "His name is Judd... J-U-D-D ... Judd." You've got to be kidding me? I'd gotten it the first time; he didn't need to spell it *and* repeat it. If I wasn't feeling so heavy at the time, it would have been funny. I did roll my eyes though to let God know I got the message. So there we were going down to the bottom of the Grand Canyon: my new husband, myself, and Judd, my alter-ego donkey. I couldn't have been more stressed out, and my husband couldn't have been more blissed out. His head often turned up to the sky, enjoying his experience completely.

We eventually got to the bottom of the Grand Canyon, staying overnight at Phantom Ranch. I wish I could remember that experience, but I wasn't present for it. In the morning when it was time to go back up, I was convinced I needed an airlift. Every muscle was seized up. I couldn't move. I was so stressed out from holding onto that donkey it felt like I'd imploded. Of course my husband was still blissful, obviously confused about why I wasn't enjoying the honeymoon. "I want my mom."

I insisted the tour guide call a helicopter, at my expense, but he wasn't having it. He put me back on Judd and held the reins all the way up the canyon. I was a sack of potatoes on the back of that poor donkey. Once in a while I'd unwind enough to look around at the canyon for a second or two. Then I'd collapse back onto Judd. Not surprisingly, I don't remember much.

After the Grand Canyon we went to live in Southern California with his mother, in the middle of nowhere — way down a dirt road with no neighbors except dismal mountains surrounding the house. Those mountains surrounded me and kept in all the fear I was experiencing. The fact I was spending most of my free time in the fetal position, rocking back and forth, was a solid indication I wasn't doing well. Both of us were dysfunctional enough at the time to not be able to communicate our needs. He did wonder why I wasn't doing well. The only thing I could come up with to assuage his concerns, was I missed living in the ashram. He bought it, thinking I would get over it.

I can't remember how long I stayed there, because finally my self-preservation kicked in — I bolted. Not yet able to end a two-month-old marriage. I made arrangements to return to

Northern California. I'd stay in the ashram there and look for a job. Once I had an apartment my husband would come. I remember climbing on the train, my husband waving at me from the platform. He looked confused, disappointed, and sad. I just felt relieved.

Finally aware I had issues, I'd started a five-year relationship with my new husband. That proved to be a sure-fire way to flush those issues out. Ultimately divorce couldn't be avoided. After our divorce we stayed friends for a while. It was through my ex-husband I was introduced to many alternative healing modalities. He was a major player in my becoming aware of my issues, and then with the tools he brought into my life, in releasing those issues.

All relationships are designed to show us where we're still holding onto the ego's wrong-minded thoughts. We've all lived through some incredible stories. In my case this relationship wasn't healthy enough to stay in. The healthy thing was to *not* be in it. There are many relationships where love is actually present and yet the ego-mind will look for ways for people to fight. Whatever we decide, it's the feelings we're left with which are what we need to look at. What's coming up? Is it true? Who is speaking?

Once we choose as always which inner teacher we're going to learn from, we can communicate with our partners or family members. Depending on which teacher you choose, the outcome will be quite different. Had I continued listening to the wrong-minded thoughts, ego thoughts, I would have stayed with him and fought out our differences and lived a life of misery. In finally being able to choose right-minded thoughts, by listening to my Higher Self, it put me on a completely different trajectory of life. Even though I still had a lot to work out, it set me on a healthier path.

CHAPTER 10

The Ego's Junk Drawers

The unexamined life is not worth living.
- SOCRATES -

YOU KNOW the feeling, like you've just gotten kicked in the gut, or there's just free-floating anxiety? You may feel fear, shame, etc. The list, as we know, goes on. The ego-mind has managed to store its issues for use at any time it feels you're getting too peaceful. 'Issues' get stored in the chakra system within our energetic field.

It takes awareness to notice what's happening within us. A useful tool is knowledge of the seven chakras and the energies they hold. Chakra is a Sanskrit word meaning disc or wheel. These invisible 'wheels of light' are in the subtle energy field of the body, arranged vertically along the length of the spine, with the first chakra at the base of the spine and the seventh at the crown of the head. Each chakra relates to a particular energetic realm of our physical and spiritual life.

I call the lower chakras (1st-4th) the ego's junk drawers. Whatever issues we have, the ego stuffs them away in the appropriate drawer, where wrong-minded thoughts can stagnate if not recognized and released. If it's a financial concern or sense of scarcity about anything, that goes in the first drawer or chakra. Control and boundary issues fit neatly in the third chakra. If you're too rigid, you can be too defended and people don't get to know you. If your boundaries are too loose, you can feel like a doormat. When can you say 'no' when you mean no, and say 'yes' when you mean yes, without needing to explain yourself? That would be an example of a healthy boundary. When we undo the ego-mind, we're left with a healthy way of being, there's nothing to stuff in a drawer. That would be a true healing, the letting go of who we're not. This allows our Higher Self to take precedence.

Understanding the chakras can assist our mental and physical well-being. There're many approaches to opening the chakras, which often entails clearing them of old energies (meaning old ideas, concepts, beliefs, etc). These include nutrition, crystals, herbs, sound vibration, chanting, aromatherapy, meditation, energy work, and more. Any of these can be useful to the degree that we direct focused intention on the chakras. These modalities affect the vibration of the subtle body and can shift our energy in positive ways. The only way to *keep* the chakras balanced, is to undo the ego-mind's thought system.

The Course doesn't talk about the chakra system, instead addressing wrong-minded thoughts (the ego's thought system) and right-minded thoughts (the Higher Self's thought system). The chakra system can help us understand how and where we hold onto our thoughts of separation.

At the end of this chapter, there will be a meditation. It's best to get familiar with your own issues or triggers when you do the meditation. If you aren't yet familiar with what may still be lurking in your subconscious mind, there's a description of the chakras below. Read through them and see what comes up.

Learning the Chakras

1ST • MULADHARA — Signified by the color red, the first chakra is in the area of the perineum and provides the foundation of our life. It attracts energies related to beliefs about our finances, safety and security, and sense of family, traditions, and culture. *This chakra is concerned with survival and is blocked by fears.*

Symptoms of disorder: Overly concerned with material life, money, safety and security. Sense of lack in any area of your life. Or following traditional values which don't resonate with you.

Example: When I was younger my mother begged me to have children, which was significant to her culture and family. It didn't matter that I wasn't married when she was begging me; she just wanted the assurance I would comply. I was clear I never wanted children. If I had them because of a sense of obligation, that would be a first chakra imbalance. Of course, I could be true to myself *and* love my mother without making her, or myself wrong.

Healthy expressions: Feeling safe and secure within yourself. Trusting your basic life needs are covered.

2ND • SVADHISHTHANA — Symbolized by the color orange, the second chakra governs the area of the sexual organs and has to do with movement, flow of life and passion — not only sexual passion but our passion for life, allowing for life's pleasures. It also feeds enthusiasm and creativity. *This chakra deals with pleasure and is blocked by shame.*

Symptoms of disorder: Lack of movement and flow in the body. Weak motivation or lack of creativity. Sexual issues across the spectrum from suppression to promiscuity. Not allowing life's pleasures, sexual or otherwise. Difficulty feeling connected to the senses.

Healthy expressions: An easygoing style and healthy, meaningful relationships. Instinctive enjoyment of life. Can you allow yourself a vacation, a walk in nature and feel connected to the senses?

3RD • MANIPURA — The third chakra, designated as yellow, in the area of the solar plexus. From this center emanates our personality and confidence, boundaries or lack thereof, personal will and sense of independence. *This chakra expresses willpower and is blocked by guilt.*

Symptoms of disorder: Low self-esteem, anger, egocentric will (not allowing God's will). Control issues. Anxiety, dissatisfaction, complaints, restlessness.

Healthy expressions: A calm centeredness, inner peace, allowing others their differences.

4TH • ANAHATA — Signified by the color green, the fourth chakras is at the heart level. It's about love, compassion, forgiveness, tolerance, trust, and generosity. This is also where we may hold feelings of suspicion, sadness, depression, and resentment. *This chakra is concerned with love and blocked by grief.*

Symptoms of disorder: Anger, jealousy, suspicion of love and kindness, intolerance of others' feelings or beliefs.

Healthy expressions: Kindness, acceptance, forgiveness, considering others needs. Feeling love toward self and others.

5TH • VISHUDDHA — Pictured as blue, the fifth chakra is at the level of the throat and has to do with speaking your truth, honesty, and service to others. It also activates compassion and the ability to listen. _This chakra deals with truth and is blocked by lies._

Symptoms of disorder: Difficulty in speaking your needs without fear of retribution. Finding yourself walking on eggshells around family or friends. Speaking too fast without clarity. Not stepping up in service to others.

Healthy expressions: Clear confident speech, kindness and consideration in relating to others. Being a good listener.

6TH • AJNA — Characterized by the color indigo, the sixth chakra is at the level of the forehead between the eyes. Also called the third eye, it enables divine insight, intuition, wisdom, and inner knowledge. _This chakra deals with spiritual vision and is blocked by illusions._

Symptoms of disorder: Depression, confusion, lack of focus. Refusal or inability to heed intuition.

Healthy expressions: Clarity of mind and being. Though this chakra is also known as the chakra for clairvoyance and interdimensional seeing, it's really about seeing the world from God's point of view without the ego's commentary on what 'should' be happening. Can we let the world do what it does without judgement?

7TH • SAHASRARA — Designated as violet/white, the seventh chakra is at the crown of the head. It receives and transmits self-realization or unity consciousness. As our connection to source energy, this chakra transmits illumination. _This chakra deals with cosmic energy and is blocked by earthly attachments._

Symptoms of disorder: loss of faith, depression, listlessness. This chakra is blocked by earthly attachments and the need to be a separate individual. Depression and listlessness are the result of the ego-mind believing that we're trapped in illusion. Once we catch on to what we're not, we can progress toward knowing we _are_ our Higher Self. We are so much more than what the ego-mind wants us to realize.

Healthy expressions: Unity consciousness, spiritual equanimity, profound peace and oneness.

Many people come to Sedona for the vortex energies here. When people come for spiritual reasons it's for spiritual connection and/or for healing (letting go). On my tours, I introduce people to this amazing place, and ways to bring this energy home with them for ongoing inner transformation. There're two different vortex flows. One is an upflow, which activates the upper chakras (heart chakra to the crown chakra). The other is downflow energy, (heart chakra to the base chakra).

On the tours I first take people to an upflow location, where they can connect with the energy of their Higher Self. Then we go to the downflow area, which is a place more conducive to letting go and release. On one tour, there was a lovely couple both about 75. The husband made it clear he didn't want to be there, he was doing this for his wife. What I do is very practical and down to earth, so he relaxed and followed along. In the first stop (upflow) he really connected to God's presence, and had the realization this presence is there all the time within him.

We then went to the downflow area, which is about letting go of our ego concepts. Once we settled into this spot, he immediately got very angry and loudly announced, "I don't like it here!" I'd taken hundreds of people there before and no one had responded so fiercely.

I asked him what was going on. Still very angry, he said, "Well! Up there, (meaning the upflow), I was really happy. But here, you two (his wife and I) didn't do anything to me — but I am PISSED OFF!" His wife chimed in, "Yeah, and if you were at work, you'd be screaming at your employees!"

That one statement gave me a lot of information; he was habitually in blame mode. When he'd get triggered he'd immediately look around to blame someone for how he was feeling. Without provocation, the downflow area had activated his lower chakras where rage is stored. Rage ran his life at that time, and it flooded up into his awareness without any other trigger.

We don't like the feelings we consider negative, and look to get rid of these feelings by projecting onto others. That doesn't make us feel better, but it seems to justify how we feel: *"It's those people who make me feel this way!"*

When I realized what was happening with him, I described how energies arise within us. We label them with a story and look around for the cause. That's what people do all the time, they project their feelings onto others. As I spoke about projection, he got it. Still feeling the rage, he looked at me and said. "Yeah, but *now* what do I do with it?" That statement showed he was willing to see things differently, and let go.

I asked him to access his experience from our first stop when he felt his connection *with* God. Then, from that perspective, we looked at the energy of rage. (You can't let go of who you think you are, unless you know who you *actually* are). I suggested he fully feel the energy of rage, welcoming it, without resistance and without judgment. Instead, breathing through it — in other words, letting God look at the rage *with* him. After only two minutes, very surprised, he said "OH!" I asked him what happened, and he said, "It's gone!"

Now, did he let go of all his rage at that moment? Probably not. But he had the experience that energy just comes up within us, to be released, not projected. Even if every other time, rage came up in him, instead of blaming others, he now has a choice. He could welcome it and allow it without judgment. Eventually he could say, he *used to be* a rageful man. However when he's projecting onto the outside world, then the outside world is his reality, rather than his inner world.

EXERCISE:

Based on the preceding chakra descriptions, write down what beliefs you're holding, and which chakras they're stored in. You don't have to focus on any one chakra — let the list prompt you to introspection, reflection, and letting go. You can't let go of anything until you're aware of it.

Look at the chakras again, especially the underlined notes to prompt what may still be hidden in the ego's junk drawers.

Once you're aware of something, that's the opportunity for freedom.

CHAKRA 1

_____

_____

_____

CHAKRA 2

_____

_____

_____

CHAKRA 3

_____

_____

_____

CHAKRA 4

_____

_____

_____

CHAKRA 5

_____

_____

_____

CHAKRA 6

_____

_____

_____

CHAKRA 7

_____

_____

_____

For me, the ego-mind expressed itself as rage. Maybe for you, it shows up as shame, depression, or anxiety. There are several ways to work with what you've written down. Choose any of the processes you've read about. The basic strategy is to recognize the energy of what comes up, welcome it without judgment, and look at it *with* the Higher Self, as in the story above.

You can also use this meditation:

MEDITATION

Get comfortable, sitting up or reclining, whichever feels best. Rest your hands on top of each other on your lap, palms facing down, with index fingers and thumbs touching. Take a deep inhalation for four counts, and exhale on a longer count of six.

Again, another full inhalation to the count of four and fully out on the count of six. Now continue breathing at your own rhythm, allowing every breath you take to relax your body and your mind. Allow yourself to BE the expression of Higher Self, or God.

From this level of perception, you can release. Look from above the issue and notice how easy it is now to let go.

If random thoughts arise, let them go. The mind can only do one thing at a time: Think, or focus. When you find yourself thinking thoughts not related to this meditation, gently come back to the breath.

In this meditation let what you discovered from the chakras come up into your awareness. With total welcoming, allow each thought to arise.

As you continue to relax, allow yourself to be aware of old thoughts and old patterns you discovered in the chakras. Know they're *not* who you are. They arise from energy stored in the subtle body being used by the conditioned ego-mind to keep us believing we're something we are not.

Any feeling or emotion which comes up can be released with the awareness of Higher Self. There's nothing inherently right or wrong about a feeling or belief; it just is.

As you look at what is coming up — observe without judgment. Let everything come up, handing it over to Higher Self and watching it dissolve back into love.

Continue breathing through any feelings, and allow yourself to come back to peace.

Stay quiet for as long as you'd like, and when you're ready, wiggle your fingers and toes and open your eyes.

CHAPTER 11

Who Are We Anyway?

Who looks outside, dreams. Who looks inside, awakens.

- CARL JUNG -

I T'S BEEN said spiritual work doesn't even begin until we start to ask the question "Who am I?" So many concepts have to be let go of before we can consider seriously contemplating this. We first have to realize we aren't the egos we've identified with.

At first we believe we're a body, thinking thoughts, and believing those thoughts are actually us. Those thoughts get backed up by feelings, all of which have powerful stories behind them. All thoughts and feelings give proof to the ego that it's real. Then comes the ego's insistence it knows what's right for itself and everyone else. Anyone who disagrees is simply wrong.

The next belief (realization, really) is, "I'm more than a body, I'm an individual soul." Body identification is still strong here. The ego is still very involved at that stage of realization; it's taken on a more spiritual persona. It still needs to be right and assert it's spirituality is more advanced than other egos. Useful inner work can be done at this stage, by beginning to clear out concepts and judgments. There's still a 'me' which is getting better and evolving. There's a 'me' that's going to get enlightened.

Eventually comes the realization we're awareness, aware we're all dreaming. We're now choosing to identify as our Higher Self and we're more willing *not* to believe and identify with the ego-mind. Following that, one can choose to relinquish individual identity entirely. This is called enlightenment or oneness.

All of this isn't a linear evolution. We'll jump back and forth between these stages. Any spiritual person can still get involved with believing this world is the real world. But they'll spend less and less time with the ego-mind. It takes strengthening our inner awareness to step out of the ego-mind. Though it's easy to fall back into conditioning. This back-and-forth process is part of undoing the ego-mind. Our inner awareness improves as we become more vigilant, recognizing our triggers and emotions, which only block love's presence.

Sometimes there are people who suddenly wake up. Consider Eckhart Tolle, a spiritual teacher and author. Eckhart went to bed one night seriously considering suicide after being depressed for thirty years. He felt he couldn't live with himself anymore. The next morning he woke free from the ego-mind. He had no idea what had happened. He was awestruck by this astonishing new state. He'd gone to sleep thinking, "Who is this '*me*' that '*I*' can no longer live with?" He realized he was more than his ego-mind, much more. It felt to him as if there was something else present within him.

Eckhart experienced what some spiritual teachers call a 'freebie.' His experience is rare. For most of us there's inner work:

letting go of our habitual attachments to certain thoughts and feelings. Then we learn to choose where we want our attention to go.

On one level someone could look at Eckhart and decide he needed therapy, because he was so consumed by this ego-mind and depression. Yet in his case one epiphany changed his entire world. Like Eckhart, we don't have to heal everything in the ego-mind. This idea can keep us continually working on ourselves. There's nothing to fix. It's the identification with the ego-mind we're releasing. Without warning, Eckhart woke up with all his ego-mind conditioning being released. We're doing the same thing, just a little more slowly.

It doesn't matter where we're at, spiritually speaking, or where we think we are. Stages of progress fluctuate, so there's no way to tell where 'you' are on the path. This idea of knowing where 'you' are, spiritually speaking, is the ego's question. But if you had to guess where you're at, think about how quickly you can let go of a grievance and forgive yourself for buying into the ego-mind's point of view.

We collect so many impressions along the way in our lifetimes. We come into our present life with certain ideas, judgments, and a reservoir of guilt already intact. It's like we've come in with a suitcase full of fears from other lifetimes (which, yup, did get stored in the ego's junk drawers). The ego's thrilled we've come back with our fear, ready for another go: we get captured by the sheer intensity of ego-driven experiences.

One more time — not every hurt and wound you've experienced has to be 'healed.' That's an ego trick to keep us busy making sure we think we're healing. Since there's so much to heal and fix in our lives, we'll be busy forever; keeping our attention on what's not necessary. It gives us the feeling we're getting better, evolving, and getting closer to God. This keeps us so busy that we don't have the time or energy to actually *let go* and wake up.

Who Do You Think You Are?

Let's take a look at some of the things we identify with.

Write down ten ways in which you identify yourself: I am a parent, I am a doctor, etc. Write them all down.

_____

_____

_____

Take a look at what you wrote. Is this list really you, or just the roles you play in your life? We identify without even considering any other possibilities. We've changed considerably over the years. Our bodies are different, our roles even change. What is the one constant? Look at the exercises below and see which resonates with you. It's a great practice to do as you can throughout your day. Just a second here and another second there.

EXERCISES:

1) Before you took on any adult roles, you were a child. Imagine yourself as an infant, pre-verbal, without any role or identity. You're responding only to sensations and feelings. Imagine now you can step into being an infant, and experience what it might be like. Who knows this? Who experiences this? Imagine your-

self as an infant looking around the room, observing people as they care for you. You're just being, there's no separation from what's happening in the moment. Ask yourself who or what is looking, without labeling or judging?

2) Begin by looking at something out your window. Look at it with soft eyes and imagine you take a step back within yourself (being aware of what is aware). Be aware of what or who is looking. Bring that awareness second by second into your life. What's watching you play all your current roles?

3) Imagine you are one with God. Where's the suffering now? Close your eyes, and breathe into that awareness. Allow your breath to expand the space within yourself. When we can do this our feeling of being on guard disappears, and our breathing will become deeper, more even. There's a more expansive view as we take everything in. It's quiet, there're no thoughts. You can step back and be aware of what is aware.

Practice one of these ideas several times a day for a few seconds or more. Choose to leave the conditioned mind for several seconds at a time, as often as you can throughout the day. It's a good way to begin easing out of the ego-mind.

**Imagine you are one with God —
Where's the suffering now?**

CHAPTER 12

Seriously, Merlin?

We can never obtain peace in the outer world
until we make peace with ourselves.
- HIS HOLINESS THE 14TH DALAI LAMA -

KEN WAPNICK, a teacher of *A Course in Miracles*, once said: "Just watch a movie to see how quickly you choose sides." Even though you know a film is fiction, that doesn't stop you from getting angry when the good guy gets hurt and the bad guy wins. Or feeling wonderful at the end when the bad guy loses.

Listen — enjoy your movies — have a great time with Netflix. React away — that's part of the fun. When we're aware of our reactions, we can then better understand their origins: those reactions come from our conditioning, our opinions, our belief in right/wrong, good/bad — in short, our whole-hearted belief in duality. We believe it and we love it, even when we hate it. We're attached to our way of thinking about things. We're constantly making the outside world more real than the inside world.

I got involved in the TV series about a young Merlin. Merlin is usually portrayed as a sage or wise magician, but in this series he was still learning and making colossal mistakes. He acted against his greater wisdom often, and eventually brought down the very kingdom he was supposedly loyal to. There was an evil sorceress who personified all the characteristics of ego, using her ill will to destroy everything.

Merlin could have killed her several times, but didn't. He was even warned by a magical dragon that unless she died, chaos would reign and bring about the fall of Camelot. I found myself screaming at the screen, "Kill her!" Every time she had the advantage I'd yell at Merlin, "This is all your fault!" When I saw myself doing this, I realized I had the energy of both blame and murderous desire, echoing the ego's desire to do away with its apparent enemies.

This attachment to how we feel doesn't disappear when we watch HBO. It's simply another medium to project our subconscious guilt onto. As a matter of fact, it's a great medium to see what's hiding in our subconscious mind. We've been very appropriately socialized to not show our outright anger, but it's there. Watch where it shows up. Again I'm not saying we shouldn't enjoy movies, just notice what comes up, because it's not coming from the screen. It's coming from us. So watching the news may be a great way to see what inner work still could be done.

We get ourselves wrapped up in the illusion of our own life as easily as we do a movie. We think our own life is real and everything around us equally real. Yet our so-called 'real life' is no more than an illusion. Remember my dream of Ramana Maharshi reminding me I was too much in the story?

As I watch my reactions to movies or the news, they show me where I am still in the story, and not yet free. It's an opportunity to see where I'm still hooked into chaos. Enjoy all the emotions which come up during a movie, and notice when you're taking them seriously. Notice when you're enraged at injustice or you're frustrated with a character's behavior. Especially in documentaries which evoke pain in you, use your own reactions to see what inner work there is to do.

ACIM suggests we can place ourselves "above the battleground," that is, being above the ego's dream world of separation and division. It's an appropriate description for the world of today and throughout history. This is a planet of war, taking place on the battlegrounds within our own consciousness. I've mentioned before the ego is mostly 'fight' energy. It doesn't care who it fights with. It may be people we hate or those we love the most. It simply prefers unrest. Practicing being above the battleground means being the observer of the world, (even when watching shows).

Of course something will always happen on the world stage so horrific you feel you must pick a side. Vicious wars, attacks and attempts at conquest occur regularly. Once you've chosen a side, you're in the war. We can't help but feel the pain which comes up. But it's possible for us to see everyone, victims and victimizers alike, as dream characters who are so captive within their stories they have no choice but to play their parts. In rising above the battleground, we can be the observer, and forgive ourselves for believing the dream.

Condoning horrible behavior, or dismissing it since it's *only* Maya or illusion, would be a great way to indulge in 'spiritual bypassing.' Since we believe this world is real, to deny it would be bypassing. What's our reaction to this dream world? That's what we look to release. If a disturbance comes up, feel it, welcome it, accept it and let it go. If you're called to do something, *do something*, however seemingly small. Most of us are not called to act on the world stage, yet we contribute by how we view the world. Remember the Butterfly Effect. As we see the world from Higher Self, right-minded thoughts, we wake ourselves up from the dream, bringing others along with us.

How many peace activists use wrong-minded thoughts and actually send hate to their opposition? Those who are called to work on the world stage can connect and interact usefully by following right-minded thoughts. What that looks like is intervening to help a cause without making the perpetrator wrong for what they're doing. Remember if they could do better they would. We can look at everyone involved in a conflict as calling out for love.

Inhumane events have always happened. How can you hate one side of an issue, over the other side without jumping into their reality? There's no quick fix. It's our individual transformation which affects everyone's experience on this earth.

Which inner teacher we bring to the work we do in the world will bring a different intention and therefore a different outcome. We're all fighting an inner battle, the ageless struggle between good and evil. Trite, but true. We can recognize our confusion and lack of peace comes from this inner battle, which is visible everywhere, even in the movies.

"There is no safety in a battleground. You can look down on it in safety from above and not be touched. But from within it you can find no safety. Not one tree left still standing will shelter you."[1]

The safety we want is never in the world. It's always right here in the choice for our right-minded thoughts. The world itself may never change, but we'll change. We can change how we see things, just one second at a time.

"Those with the strength of God in their awareness could never think of battle. What could they gain but loss of their perfection? For everything fought for on the battleground is of the body; ... No one who knows that he has everything could seek for limitation, nor could he value the body's offerings. The senselessness of conquest is quite apparent from the quiet sphere above the battleground." [2]

The senselessness of conquest can be recognized anytime we want to be right in our opinions, beliefs, concepts, and judgements of self and 'others.' It's okay for all these thoughts to show up (cuz they're gonna). They're coming up to be cleared. It's surrender, it's letting go. Not the ego's idea of surrender, which is giving up into victimhood. But surrender, letting go into your next stage of deeper connection with God. This sets us free from the perceived limitations we have (up until now) believed.

CHAPTER 13

Jesus And Buddha Weren't Bliss Ninnies

Be in the world, but not of it.

- JESUS -

MANY people when first on the spiritual path feel relieved their earthly problems have a solution. This is where for some, the idea of spiritual bypassing happens. There's such a strong desire to be free they bypass the work and stay in a fabricated bliss state. They don't immediately realize it, but the ego-mind has thrown them a curveball.

This is what is called a bliss ninny: someone who seems intoxicated with spirituality, but is not grounded in the teachings. They want to vibrate off the planet into spirit, or feel bliss all the time. If only that were enough...

I saw a documentary about the Guru Meher Baba. Meher Baba was an Indian spiritual master who left his body in 1969. In this documentary, he was going around west-central India, near the city of Ahmednagar, bringing sadhus (a holy man, sage, or ascetic), out of samadhi (a state of consciousness where one is experiencing oneness with the divine).

When the documentary was over, I asked someone why he did that? I mean, wasn't that the entire point of spiritual work and something I seriously wanted for myself? It was explained he was bringing these sadhus out of deep meditation because they hadn't finished their inner work. They were lost in their upper chakras experiencing constant bliss. If they left the world without completing their inner work, they'd have to come back. Meher Baba was doing them a favor.

There're so many examples of great beings on this planet, from different cultures and religions. They all did their inner work. They all stopped believing and identifying with the ego-mind and became identified with their true self. Two great beings most of us are familiar with are Jesus and Buddha.

Buddha was born a wealthy prince and lived in a palace. His name was Siddhartha Gautama, a wealthy prince. At his birth, it was predicted he'd be a great spiritual master or a great king. His father wanted him to be a great king. He wanted to protect Siddhartha from the suffering of the world, which he worried would prompt deep introspection and questioning 'reality.' Siddhartha's life was spent inside the palace grounds, where he fell in love and got married. As life would have it, despite his father's attempts to prepare him for his reign as a king, he had a deep inner calling for more.

Eventually he wandered away from the palace, leaving all the wealth and the love of his wife behind. He saw for himself the suffering of people who were poor, sick, and dying. This did indeed prompt deep contemplation. After seeing a monk meditating, he recognized the truth was within Siddhartha himself, not in the world or its riches, or poverty. He renounced his position and tried many inner pathways to enlightenment with different teachers and techniques.

He finally settled on the 'middle way', and awakened from the ego-mind. He began teaching the middle way, which is the path between extreme renunciation of the world (since ascetics felt the world was not real), and complete indulgence in the body.

Another great being is Jesus. We all know the story where he went into the desert and fasted for 40 days and 40 nights. During that time the devil (ego) came to Jesus and tempted him. The temptations were lust, (temptations of the body) egoism, (pride of life) and materialism (the riches of the world). Whether those 40 days and nights actually happened or were meant to be a metaphor for the intensity of the situation, what was he doing for 40 days and 40 nights?

Jesus was doing the same thing we're being asked to do. He was dealing with the last vestiges of the ego-mind. He finally let it all go into his God-mind, and completely released the illusion of the world. The world could no longer ensnare him. He was at peace — no longer identified with the body. He knew he was pure spirit.

Jesus and Buddha weren't bliss ninnies hiding out in their upper chakras. They did the work, released identification with the ego-mind, and discovered who they truly were. They were completely present, no longer identified with the ego's shenanigans.

They both then turned around and started teaching us how to free ourselves. When Jesus taught 'I AM' the way, he didn't mean him personally, but the 'I AM' presence in every one of us. That's where he was pointing us to, the 'I AM' presence.

At one point he said: "Be on this earth but not of it." That's the point of doing our spiritual practices. Once we are fully identified with our God-Self, we'll still occupy this body, but our identification will be with God. The drama of the world is now seen as the workings of the ego-identified mind.

We're all invited to let go of the ego-mind and be in the state Jesus and Buddha lived in throughout their lives. We all have inner work to do, until we don't.

The holy instant does not come from your little willingness alone. It is always the result of your small willingness combined with the unlimited power of God's Will.[1]

Your small willingness to choose otherwise, just one second at a time, is met with God's greater will for our success. We get to choose.

In a workshop I attended, the teacher guided us into a meditation bringing us into our inner presence of God. We were to ask a question, or ask for guidance. At that point in the meditation I simply said: "I want to stay with you." The answer which came back to me was:

"Then stay with me."
How do I do that?

Just one second at a time.

For private Spiritual Mentoring
and/or Spiritual Journey Tours
in Sedona, Arizona with
Vishali Shahin

Visit:

SedonaHealingJourney.com

or

VishaliShahin.com

On either website, go to:
Offerings

In-person sessions or via Zoom

Suggested Reading

1) *A Course in Miracles* 3rd edition, published by The Foundation For Inner Peace (Mill Valley, Ca: Foundation for Inner Peace, 2007) ACIM.org

2) *The Disappearance of the Universe* by Gary Renard

3) *Where Are You Going?* by Swami Muktananda

4) *Autobiography of a Yogi* by Paramahansa Yogananda

5) *Siddhartha* by Herman Hesse

6) *The Surrender Experiment* by Michael A. Singer

7) *Silence of the Heart* by Robert Adams

8) *When Fear Falls Away* by Jan Frazer

9) *Healing the Unhealed Mind* by Kenneth Wapnick, Ph. D.

10) *A Course in Health and Well Being* by Cindy Lora-Renard

11) *A Thousand Names for Joy* by Byron Katie

12) *end your story. Begin your life...* by Jim Dreaver

13) *The Myth of Enlightenment* by Karl Renz

14) *The Untethered Soul* by Michael A. Singer

15) *What's On My Mind* by Swami Anantananda

A Course in Miracles
QUOTE REFERENCES

A Course in Miracles consists of three parts: the Text, Workbook for Students, and Manual for Teachers. This annotation system for the quotes was devised by the publisher, The Foundation for Inner Peace: T (Text), W (Workbook), or M (Manual for Teachers) followed by chapter, workbook lesson, section, paragraph.

To fully understand the annotation system please refer to ACIM.org and search for 'annotations.'

CHAPTER 2
1. T-27.VIII 6

CHAPTER 3
1. T-2.VI
2. W-68
3. W-69
4. T-6 V-C

CHAPTER 5
1. T-13s

CHAPTER 7
1. W-p.II. 1.1:1-7

CHAPTER 8
1. W-132 5:1-3
2. W-16.2:3

CHAPTER 12
1. T-23.III.6:4-8
2. T-23.IV.9:1-5

CHAPTER 13
1. T-18.IV.4